Teaching Literacy Skills to Adolescents Using CORETTA SCOTT KING Award Winners

Carianne Bernadowski, PhD

A LINWORTH PUBLISHING BOOK

LIBRARIES UNLIMITED
An Imprint of ABC-CLIO, LLC

A B C ● C L I O

Santa Barbara, California • Denver, Colorado • Oxford, England

Library of Congress Cataloging-in-Publication Data

Bernadowski, Carianne.
  Teaching literacy skills to adolescents using Coretta Scott King Award winners / Carianne Bernadowski.
  p. cm.
"A Linworth Publishing book."
Includes bibliographical references and index.
ISBN-13: 978-1-58683-337-4 (pbk.)
ISBN-10: 1-58683-337-5 (pbk.)
1. Language arts (Secondary)--United States. 2. Young adult literature, American--Study and teaching (Secondary) 3. African Americans in literature--Study and teaching (Secondary) 4. African American teenagers--Books and reading--United States. 5. African American teenagers--Education. 6. Coretta Scott King Award. I. Title.
LB1631.B393 2009
428.0071'2--dc22   2009015279

13 12 11 10 9   1 2 3 4 5

This book is also available on the World Wide Web as an eBook.
Visit www.abc-clio.com for details.

ABC-CLIO, LLC
130 Cremona Drive, P.O. Box 1911
Santa Barbara, California 93116-1911

This book is printed on acid-free paper ∞
Manufactured in the United States of America

Table of Contents

Table of Figures vi

About the Author vii

Acknowledgments vii

Dedication vii

Introduction viii

    Background on the Book's Development viii

    Coretta Scott King Award. x

    Research Findings on Books Written by African-American Authors. xi

    What Works: Integrating Literature with Research-Based Literacy Strategies xii

    Coretta Scott King Award Winners: 1970-2008 xiii

    NCTE/IRA Standards for English Language Arts xv

    Information Literacy Standards for Student Learning xvi

    Standards Alignment Chart xvii

PART 1: AWARD-WINNING BOOK SELECTIONS 1

CHAPTER 1: I Never Had It Made: The Autobiography of Jackie Robinson 3
Author(s): Jackie Robinson, as told to Alfred Duckett

    Bibliographic Information 3

    Annotation 3

    Grade Level/ISBN 3

    Discussion Starters/Writing Prompts/Pre-Reading Activities 4

    Literacy Strategies for During Reading 9

    Post-Reading Activities 10

    Additional Information about the Author. 13

    Additional Resources 15

CHAPTER 2: The Young Landlords 17
Author: Walter Dean Myers

    Bibliographic Information 17

    Annotation 17

    Grade Level/ISBN 17

    Discussion Starters/Writing Prompts/Pre-Reading Activities 18

    Literacy Strategies for During Reading 19

    Post-Reading Activities 19

    Additional Information about the Author. 22

    Additional Resources 24

CHAPTER 3: Everett Anderson's Goodbye
Author: Lucille Clifton

    Bibliographic Information 25

    Annotation 25

    Grade Level/ISBN 25

    Discussion Starters/Writing Prompts/Pre-Reading Activities 26

    Literacy Strategies for During Reading 26

    Post-Reading Activities 26

    Additional Information about the Author. 30

    Additional Resources 31

CHAPTER 4: The People Could Fly: American Black Folktales 33
Author: Virginia Hamilton
      Bibliographic Information 33
      Annotation 33
      Grade Level/ISBN 33
      Discussion Starters/Writing Prompts/Pre-Reading Activities 35
      Literacy Strategies for During Reading 36
      Post-Reading Activities 36
      Additional Information about the Author. 43
      Additional Resources 44

CHAPTER 5: Justin and the Best Biscuits in the World 45
Author: Mildred Pitts Walter
      Bibliographic Information 45
      Annotation 45
      Grade Level/ISBN 45
      Discussion Starters/Writing Prompts/Pre-Reading Activities 46
      Literacy Strategies for During Reading 51
      Post-Reading Activities 51
      Additional Information about the Author. 57
      Additional Resources 57

CHAPTER 6: Fallen Angels 59
Author: Walter Dean Myers
      Bibliographic Information 59
      Annotation 59
      Grade Level/ISBN 59
      Discussion Starters/Writing Prompts/Pre-Reading Activities 60
      Literacy Strategies for During Reading 62
      Post-Reading Activities 67
      Additional Information about the Author. 70
      Additional Resources 70

CHAPTER 7: The Road to Memphis 71
Author: Mildred D. Taylor
      Bibliographic Information 71
      Annotation 71
      Grade Level/ISBN 71
      Discussion Starters/Writing Prompts/Pre-Reading Activities 72
      Literacy Strategies for During Reading 74
      Post-Reading Activities 77
      Additional Information about the Author. 83
      Additional Resources 83

CHAPTER 8: Toning the Sweep 85
Author: Angela Johnson
      Bibliographic Information 85
      Annotation 85
      Grade Level/ISBN 85
      Discussion Starters/Writing Prompts/Pre-Reading Activities 86
      Literacy Strategies for During Reading 91
      Post-Reading Activities 91
      Additional Information about the Author. 92
      Additional Resources 92

CHAPTER 9: Slam! 95
Author: Walter Dean Myers
     Bibliographic Information 95
     Annotation 95
     Grade Level/ISBN 95
     Discussion Starters/Writing Prompts/Pre-Reading Activities 96
     Literacy Strategies for During Reading 99
     Post-Reading Activities 100
     Additional Information about the Author. 100
     Additional Resources 102

CHAPTER 10: Heaven 103
Author: Angela Johnson
     Bibliographic Information 103
     Annotation 103
     Grade Level/ISBN 103
     Discussion Starters/Writing Prompts/Pre-Reading Activities 104
     Literacy Strategies for During Reading 106
     Post-Reading Activities 106
     Additional Information about the Author. 107
     Additional Resources 107

CHAPTER 11: The First Part Last 109
Author: Angela Johnson
     Bibliographic Information 109
     Annotation 109
     Grade Level/ISBN 109
     Discussion Starters/Writing Prompts/Pre-Reading Activities 110
     Literacy Strategies for During Reading 110
     Post-Reading Activities 113
     Additional Information about the Author. 118
     Additional Resources 118

CHAPTER 12: Copper Sun 119
Author: Sharon M. Draper
     Bibliographic Information 119
     Annotation 119
     Grade Level/ISBN 119
     Discussion Starters/Writing Prompts/Pre-Reading Activities 120
     Literacy Strategies for During Reading 120
     Post-Reading Activities 123
     Additional Information about the Author. 124
     Additional Resources 124

PART 2: CORETTA SCOTT KING HONOR BOOKS 125

Bibliography 133

Author Index 135

Title Index 135

Subject Index 136

Table of Figures

Figure CB1 CCBC: Children's Books by and about People of Color
Published in the U.S. from 1994-2006 xii

Figure CSK1: Coretta Scott King Author Awards from 1970-2008 xiv

Figure SC1: Standards Alignment Chart xvii

Figure 1.1: KWLQ 5

Figure 1.2: 5 W's Graphic Organizer 7

Figure 1.3: Sports Reporting Rubric 8

Figure 1.4: Collaboration Checksheet 11

Figure 1.5: Postage Stamp Rubric 12

Figure 1.6: Hero Writing Assignment Rubric 14

Figure 2.1: Business Letter Rubric 20

Figure 2.2: Neighborhood Picture Book Rubric 23

Figure 3.1: Haiku Rubric 29

Figure 4.1: Timeline Group Participation Checklist .35

Figure 4.2: Award Seal Rubric 37

Figure 4.3: Story Map 39

Figure 4.4: Folktale Rubric 40

Figure 4.5: Slave Narrative Rubric 42

Figure 5.1: Research Process Rubric 47

Figure 5.2: Oral Presentation Rubric 48

Figure 5.3: Family Tree Template 50

Figure 5.4: Literal vs. Inferential Meaning 52

Figure 5.5: Venn diagram 54

Figure 5.6: Dust Cover Checklist 56

Figure 6.1: KWL Chart 61

Figure 6.2: Character Map 63

Figure 6.3: Quote Tracker 65

Figure 6.4: Photo Quote Rubric 66

Figure 6.5: Letters Home Rubric 68

Figure 7.1: Term Tracker 73

Figure 7.2: QAR Worksheet 76

Figure 7.3: Chapter Map Rubric 78

Figure 7.4: Chapter Map Example 79

Figure 7.5: Author Information Brochure Rubric 81

Figure 7.6: Booktalk Grader 82

Figure 8.1: Concept Map 87

Figure 8.2: Desert Anticipation Guide 89

Figure 8.3: Desert Anticipation Guide Answer Key 90

Figure 9.1: Literature Circle Jobs 98

Figure 9.2: Annotation Compilation Rubric 101

Figure 10.1: Comparison Chart 105

Figure 11.1: Character Conflict Chart Record 112

Figure 11.2: Editorial Rubric 115

Figure 11.3: Script Writing Rubric 117

Figure 12.1: Character List 122

Figure CSK2: Coretta Scott King Honor Books 127

About the Author

Carianne Bernadowski, PhD, is an Assistant Professor of Elementary Education at Robert Morris University in Moon Township, Pennsylvania in the School of Education and Social Sciences. She has taught elementary, secondary, and college students for the past 15 years. She holds a PhD from The University of Pittsburgh in Pittsburgh, Pennsylvania, an M.A in Reading Education from Slippery Rock University of Pennsylvania, Slippery Rock, Pennsylvania, and a B.A. in Journalism and Communications/Secondary Education from Point Park College, Pittsburgh, Pennsylvania. Currently, she teaches literacy courses at the undergraduate and graduate levels. She continues to work with school districts in the area of literacy. She has also co-authored a book for Linworth Publishing titled *Teaching with Books that Heal: Using Authentic Literacy and Literacy Strategies to Help Children Cope with Everyday Problems.* She has written for *Library Media Connection, PA Reads, Reading Today, The Reading Professor, Teaching K-8,* and *Teaching Tolerance.*

When she is not writing or teaching, Dr. Bernadowski enjoys spending time with her three-year-old son, Maxwell, three-month-old son, Liam, and her husband, Brian. They make their home in Monroeville, Pennsylvania.

Acknowledgments

I wish to gratefully acknowledge Barbara Holtz for her dedication as a librarian and an extraordinary resource during the writing of this book. Your knowledge of the teen genre is amazing and I appreciate all of your help.

Dedication

I dedicate this book to my family, Brian, Maxwell, and Liam Bernadowski. I thank God every day that I have you to grace my life. I cannot imagine any success without you by my side. Thank you for making my life better, brighter, and worth getting up each morning.

INTRODUCTION

Background on the Book's Development

As a middle school language arts teacher for 10 years, I knew the importance of providing my students with quality literature to which they could relate. Much of the literature read by my students was dictated by a curriculum far removed from their lives. Something had to change in order for my students to connect to text they valued and, after many years, I realized that the something that needed to change was me.

While enrolled in a doctoral program in literacy education, I was required to take an elective outside my department at The University of Pittsburgh. Halfheartedly, I took a graduate course in library science. The course was taught by Dr. Margaret Kimmel, who turned out to be exactly what my students and I needed. She taught me everything I needed to know about adolescent and children's literature. I fell in love with illustrations that brought the text to life. I fell in love with the words that mimicked music to my ears, and finally I realized what it meant to be a literacy teacher. I questioned my own education on several occasions after meeting Maggie Kimmel. Maggie changed my life, but more importantly, she changed the lives of my students who so desperately needed her. I instantly began to see my students in the pages of books like *Heaven* by Angela Johnson. More importantly, my students began to see themselves. Reading was valued by my students, and they were excited about books, spending endless hours reading and talking about text. As I reflect, I know in my heart that I played a large part in the success of my classroom, but I also know that, without a librarian's influence and expert knowledge, my classroom would not have been a success that year and every year since. Following that semester, I asked Maggie if I could conduct an independent study under her guidance. She agreed and the legwork for this book began. I studied the Coretta Scott King Award winners from the award's inception to present day. You are reading much of that work in this book.

Today I no longer teach those struggling, reluctant middle school readers, but I often see many of them on the college campus where I teach. Maggie's influence continues through my instruction of pre-service elementary teachers and her love of stories continues to flourish in my once struggling readers who are now seniors in college. I share this story of Maggie because you may be like her—you may share your love of quality literature every day with no idea how far your influence reaches. I ask you to not take that responsibility lightly and be reassured your hard work pays off more than you could possibly know.

The goal of this book and the research I did under Maggie's tutelage is to provide teachers and librarians with the tools necessary to support students in their literacy journey. By featuring works by African-American authors whose main characters reflect the lives of adolescent readers, classroom teachers and librarians can fill a need that young adults so desperately need. Hefflin writes, "If teachers continually present African-American children with texts in which the main characters are predominately animals and white people, it stands to reason that these children may begin to wonder whether they, their families, and their communities fit into the world of reading" (p. 810-811). Schools and communities in the United States are rapidly becoming more diverse populations and require practitioners that have the skill set to meet the needs of those diverse learners who enter classrooms and libraries. Harris (1990) writes, "The task confronting educators, then, is to provide all children with opportunities to hear, read, write about, and talk about literature, especially literature that affirms who they are" (p. 553). This book with help close that gap and give teachers, library media specialists, and curriculum directors a viable text to use as a teaching and reference tool when working with adolescents from diverse backgrounds.

The intended audience for this book is any adult who has the opportunity to work with adolescents and make a difference in their lives. A library media specialist will use this book to aid in the collaboration with a classroom teacher as he or she works with students who are reading a Coretta Scott King Award winner. This book will be used as a supplemental text in a college education course as colleges and universities prepare their pre-service teachers to use quality literature in their standards-based lesson plans to meet the needs of all students. This text will be used by a curriculum director to choose books for a middle or high school curriculum. Finally, this book will be a valuable resource for a library media specialist to have as he or she runs an afterschool book club or teaches a class of adolescent learners. All of the people mentioned, and parents, will benefit from using this book as a tool for navigation through the texts of our teenagers' lives. It provides discussion questions and informal lessons that can be implemented either in a formal classroom or an informal book discussion. More importantly, parents can use the discussion questions to help open the lines of communication in their own homes since many of the topics in the texts are applicable to our teenagers' lives.

This book is a much needed text to showcase African-American authors' outstanding and admirable work while giving librarians and classroom teachers tools to work with said texts. This book showcases each text and provides supporting lessons and activities to complement each selection. There are no current texts that highlight the Coretta Scott King Award winners. These are the books our adolescents are reading. One way to connect with teenagers is to connect to that which they know and can relate. This book allows that connection to occur naturally for teachers, parents, and library media specialists. Since no other texts of this type exist, this is the perfect curricular companion. This text connects great literature and easy-to-use, research-based literacy strategies, a combination that is not offered by any other current texts on the market. This practical guide can be easily implemented into an existing curriculum with ease. Furthermore, each literacy strategy includes all applicable NCTE/IRA Standards for the English Language Arts and Information Literacy Standards. This feature adds to the ease of curriculum infusion.

The book consists of three distinct parts. The Introduction provides an explanation of how the book came to fruition, an explanation of the Coretta Scott King Award, research findings gathered by the Cooperative Children's Book Center on books written by African-American writers, a table of all Coretta Scott King Award winners, a table of the books referenced in this text, and information regarding the integration of quality adolescent literature and research-based literacy strategies.

Part I: Award-Winning Book Selections includes 12 chapters. Each chapter consists of a Coretta Scott King Award book selection, the bibliographic information, an annotation, applicable grade and age level, ISBN, Discussion Starters/Writing Prompts/Pre-Reading Activities, Literacy Strategies for During Reading, Post-Reading Activities, Additional Information about the Author, and Additional Resources. Additionally, many activities have accompanying assessment tools to use in the library or classroom. A user of the book may note there is much variability between rubrics and checklists. This was done purposefully by the author with the intent that each user will and can manipulate the assessment tools to use for their own needs. For instance, if your district or school is using a standards-based writing rubric, you may find one in a chapter that is similar to what you are required to use in your school. It is the intention of the author that each person will decide what works best for their students and choose assessment tools that meet their needs and match their instructional goals. Each activity within each chapter will include the Information Literacy Standards for Student Learning and the NCTE/IRA Standards for the English Language Arts. A standards alignment chart is provided at the beginning of the book for the reader's reference.

Part II: Coretta Scott King Honor Books provides a list of awarded books. A bibliography as well as an author, title, and subject index close the book.

Coretta Scott King Award

Artist Lev Mills designed the seal found on the Coretta Scott King Award books in 1974, which served to symbolize Dr. Martin Luther King's teachings and doctrines, the purpose for which the award was founded. Today when a teacher or librarian sees that distinguished seal on the cover of a book, they know it will be "a good read" for adolescent readers. Furthermore, teachers or librarians can feel confident that the text will encompass quality characters that represent the reading population for which it is intended. Since the award's inception in the late 1960s, the seal itself has morphed. Today readers find a bronze and black seal that denotes a winner of the Coretta Scott King Award and pewter and black seal that represents an honor book. The circle on the seal represents "continuity in movement revolving from one idea to another. Within the circle is an image of a black child reading a book. The five main religious symbols below the image of the child represent nonsectarianism. The superimposed pyramid symbolizes both the strength and Atlanta University, where the award was headquartered at the time when the seal was designed. At the apex of the pyramid is a dove, symbolic of peace, one of Dr. King's doctrines. The rays shine toward peace and brotherhood" <http://www.ala.org/ala/mgrps/rts/emiert/corettascottkingbookawards/abouttheawarda/cskabout.cfm>.

The innovative idea of the Coretta Scott King Award was the brainchild of Mabel McKissick and Glyndon Greer after meeting at an American Library Association meeting in 1969. Both were school librarians who attended the conference and met John Carroll, a publisher, who suggested they begin an award to honor their hero while also honoring African-American authors and illustrators. And so the seed was planted. Working with McKissack and Carroll, Greer enlisted the help of other librarians in the New York/New Jersey area, and a committee was formed. The group decided to name the award in honor of Dr. Martin Luther King's widow, Coretta Scott King. Her dedication to continue the work of peace and brotherhood that her husband fought so hard to cherish is realized through this award.

The award began in May of 1970 when Lillie Patterson was honored for her biography entitled *Martin Luther King Jr.: Man of Peace.* Since that time, the award has become a symbol of accomplishment for both authors and illustrators. In 1974, George Ford was the first illustrator honored for his illustrations in the book *Ray Charles* by Sharon Bell Mathis. Mathis was also honored with the author award that year for the same book. Today the Coretta Scott King Award seal represents accomplishment in writing and illustrations for, what many would call, some of the best written work available for adolescent readers.

Research Findings on Books Written by African-American Authors

The Cooperative Children's Book Center (CCBC) at the University of Wisconsin at Madison documents the number of books by and about people of color published in the United States. In 1985, for instance, of 2,500 trade books that were published for children and teens, only 18 were created by African Americans. The number is a clear indication of the importance of celebrating and honoring texts that are ethnically authentic and of value for children and adolescents to read. The CCBC also collects data in relation to books written by American Indians, Asian/Pacifics and Asian Pacific Americans, and Latinos. For the purpose of this book statistics presented by the CCBC in Figure CB1 are by and about African Americans and illustrates the statistics generated from 1994 to 2006.

Figure CB1 CCBC: Children's Books by and about People of Color Published in the U.S. from 1994-2006

Year	Total Number of Estimated Books	Number of Books Received by CCBC	Books by African-American Authors	Books about African-American Authors
1994	4,500	unavailable	82	166
1995	4,500		100	167
1996	4,500		92	172
1997	4,500-5,000		88	216
1998	5,000		92	183
1999	5,000		81	150
2000	5,000-5,500		96	147
2001	5,000-5,500		99	201
2002	5,000	3,150	69	166
2003	5,000	3,200	79	171
2004	5,000	2,800	99	143
2005	5,000	2,800	75	149
2006	5,000	3,000	87	153

Originally published by Cooperative Children's Book Center (CCBC).

As the numbers so poignantly illustrate, there is a clear deficient of books written by African-American authors, as well as books written about African-American characters. For example, in 1995 there were an estimated 4,500 total number of children's books published in the United States and only 82 of those published books were written by African-American authors. Likewise, of the 4,500 books published, 166 of those books included characters that are of African-American descent. Twelve years later CCBC found approximately 5,000 children's books were published and 87 were written by African-American authors and 153 of those books were about African-American characters. These numbers clearly indicate the need for quality texts for children of African-American origins. The Coretta Scott King Award winners provide readers with quality material with which they can relate ethnically.

What Works: Integrating Quality Literature with Research-Based Literacy Strategies

Librarians and language arts teachers have been using novels or chapter books to teach literacy for a very long time, but as students change so should the professional repertoire those professionals use. This repertoire must include literature and literacy strategies that speak to adolescents of today who enter the classroom and library with varying backgrounds, needs, and skill sets. Much attention has been paid to the emerging literacy skills of elementary students, but not until recently have researchers, teachers, librarians, and even parents, called for the spotlight to shine on the growing and ever-changing literacy needs of adolescents in middle and high school. The term adolescent literacy became part of the educational lexicon in the 1990s shortly after the NCTE/IRA Standards for the English Language Arts were developed in 1996. The NCTE/IRA standards present a vision of literacy education that includes the use of print, oral, and visual language, and addresses six interrelated English language arts: reading, writing, speaking, listening, viewing, and visually representing (Finders & Hynds, 2007, p. 41). Language arts and literacy are no longer separate entities to be taught in isolation, but as parts of a whole. To teach language arts is to teach the whole child in terms of literacy skills. Adolescent literacy is unique in that children are becoming adults and need skills and strategies to function in the adult world they will soon face. With this in mind, teaching students strategies they can employ when faced with text is an invaluable tool for middle and high school students. The 1999 position statement by the International Reading Association reinforced this point when it called for emphasis on literacy instruction for adolescents: "Adolescents entering the adult workforce in the 21st century will read and write more than at any other time in human history. They will need advanced levels of literacy to perform their jobs, run their households, act as citizens, and conduct their personal lives" (Moore, Bean, Birdyshaw, & Rycik, 1999, p. 99). These needs can and should be met in the classrooms and libraries that these adolescents enter and exit each day.

Adolescent literacy of today demands that teachers and librarians reexamine their instructional design to include rich and rigorous pathways to allow students to demonstrate literacy competencies. Alvermann (2002) examined adolescent literacy instruction and discovered that students' self-efficacy and engagement with a variety of texts is an important instructional design component to consider when teaching and working with adolescent readers. Additionally, she recognized that secondary students face complicated and, sometimes, overwhelmingly difficult expository texts in content areas and students must be equipped to handle the demands of these types of texts. Consequently, students must have the appropriate background knowledge and strategies to read a variety of texts in a variety of settings and contexts. Strategies such as comprehension monitoring, text structure knowledge and know-how, the ability to ask and answer varying levels of questions, summarizing, paraphrasing, problem solving, and cooperative learning are ways that teachers and librarians can support literacy in adolescents while meeting the required state and national standards. These strategies, as well as others, are imperative for students to read strategically and for real purposes.

Strategies such as literature circles are valuable to encourage dialog and discussion of text, which are critical aspects of comprehension instruction (Gambrell & Almasi, 1998). Furthermore, many of the strategies presented in this text promote independent reading, which research indicates is the single factor most strongly associated with reading achievement and success (Anderson, Wilson, & Fielding, 1988). Finally, many of the strategies in this text promote powerful elements of collaboration and cooperative learning. Zemeimann, Daniels, and Hyde (1993) categorize cooperative learning as a best educational practice since it has the high probability of student engagement, active participation, and responsibility.

Adolescent readers must know how to read to learn. The International Reading Association Committee on Adolescent Literacy (1999) recommends that adolescent learners: read a wide variety of texts that appeal to their interests, such as the Coretta Scott King Award Winners; receive modeling and explicit instruction; work with teachers who understand the complex nature of readers; participate in assessments that determine literacy strengths and needs; and finally, receive support from home, community, and nation. That community partnership can be easily accomplished through efforts of the public library. Teachers and librarians must understand and implement quality, research-based instructional practices with adolescent learners who need guidance through their journey to literate adulthood.

Coretta Scott King Award Winners: 1970-2009

Figure CSK1 is a comprehensive list of all Coretta Scott King Award Winners from 1970 to 2009. This list is intended for use as a reference for librarians and classroom teachers. Many of these texts may already be present in your collection. Use this as a checklist for collection development.

Figure CSK1: Coretta Scott King Author Awards from 1970-2009

YEAR	TITLE	AUTHOR
2009	*We Are the Ship: The Story of Negro League Baseball*	Kadir Nelson
2008	*Elijah of Buxton*	Christopher Paul Curtis
2007	*Copper Sun*	Sharon Draper
2006	*Day of Tears: A Novel In Dialogue*	Julius Lester
2005	*Remember: The Journey to School Integration*	Toni Morrison
2004	*The First Part Last*	Angela Johnson
2003	*Bronx Masquerade*	Nikki Grimes
2002	*The Land*	Mildred D. Taylor
2001	*Miracle's Boys*	Jacqueline Woodson
2000	*Bud, Not Buddy*	Christopher Paul Curtis
1999	*Heaven*	Angela Johnson
1998	*Forged by Fire*	Sharon Draper
1997	*Slam!*	Walter Dean Myers
1996	*Her Stories: African-American Folktales, Fairy Tales, and True Tales*	Virginia Hamilton
1995	*Christmas in the Big House, Christmas in the Quarters*	Patricia and Frederick McKissack
1994	*Toning the Sweep*	Angela Johnson
1993	*Dark Thirty: Southern Tales of the Supernatural*	Patricia McKissack
1992	*Now Is Your Time: The African-American Struggle for Freedom*	Walter Dean Myers
1991	*The Road to Memphis*	Mildred D. Taylor
1990	*A Long Hard Journey: The Story of the Pullman Porter*	Patricia & Fredrick McKissack
1989	*Fallen Angels*	Walter Dean Myers
1988	*The Friendship*	Mildred D. Taylor
1987	*Justin and the Best Biscuits in the World*	Mildred Pitts Walter
1986	*The People Could Fly: American Black Folktales*	Virginia Hamilton
1985	*Motown and Didi: A Love Story*	Walter Dean Myers
1984	*Everett Anderson's Good-bye*	Lucille Clifton
1983	*Sweet Whispers, Brother Rush*	Virginia Hamilton
1982	*Let the Circle Be Unbroken*	Mildred D. Taylor
1981	*This Life*	Sidney Poitier
1980	*The Young Landlords*	Walter Dean Myers
1979	*Escape to Freedom: The Story of Young Fredrick Douglas*	Ossie Davis
1978	*Africa Dream*	Eloise Greenfield
1977	*The Story of Stevie Wonder*	James Haskins
1976	*Duey's Tale*	Pearl Bailey
1975	*The Legend of Africana*	Dorothy Robinson
1974	*Ray Charles*	Sharon Bell Mathis
1973	*I Never Had It Made: The Autobiography of Jackie Robinson*	Jackie Robinson, as told to Alfred Duckett
1972	*17 Black Artists*	Elton C. Fax
1971	*Black Troubador: Langston Hughes*	Charlemae Rollins
1970	*Martin Luther King, Jr.: Man of Peace*	Lillie Patterson

Reprinted with permission from the American Library Association.

Each activity included in this book contains a reference to the Standards for the English Language Arts sponsored by the National Council for the Teaching of English/International Reading Association and the Information Literacy Standards for Student Learning. Both set of standards are national standards and serve as a framework for driving quality instruction in reading/language arts and information literacy.

NCTE/IRA Standards for the English Language Arts

1. Students read a wide range of print and non-print texts to build an understanding of texts, of themselves, and of the cultures of the United States and the world; to acquire new information; to respond to the needs and demands of society and the workplace; and for personal fulfillment. Among these texts are fiction and nonfiction, classic and contemporary works.

2. Students read a wide range of literature from many periods in many genres to build an understanding of the many dimensions (e.g., philosophical, ethical, aesthetic) of human experience.

3. Students apply a wide range of strategies to comprehend, interpret, evaluate, and appreciate texts. They draw on their prior experience, their interactions with other readers and writers, their knowledge of word meaning and of other texts, their word identification strategies, and their understanding of textual features (e.g., sound-letter correspondence, sentence structure, context, graphics).

4. Students adjust their use of spoken, written, and visual language (e.g., conventions, style, vocabulary) to communicate effectively with a variety of audiences and for different purposes.

5. Students employ a wide range of strategies as they write and use different writing process elements appropriately to communicate with different audiences for a variety of purposes.

6. Students apply knowledge of language structure, language conventions (e.g., spelling and punctuation), media techniques, figurative language, and genre to create, critique, and discuss print and non-print texts.

7. Students conduct research on issues and interests by generating ideas and questions, and by posing problems. They gather, evaluate, and synthesize data from a variety of sources (e.g., print and non-print texts, artifacts, people) to communicate their discoveries in ways that suit their purpose and audience.

8. Students use a variety of technological and information resources (e.g., libraries, databases, computer networks, video) to gather and synthesize information and to create and communicate knowledge.

9. Students develop an understanding of and respect for diversity in language use, patterns, and dialects across cultures, ethnic groups, geographic regions, and social roles.

10. Students whose first language is not English make use of their first language to develop competency in the English language arts and to develop understanding of content across the curriculum.

11. Students participate as knowledgeable, reflective, creative, and critical members of a variety of literacy communities.

12. Students use spoken, written, and visual language to accomplish their own purposes (e.g., for learning, enjoyment, persuasion, and the exchange of information)

Standards for the English Language Arts, by the International Reading Association and National Council for Teachers of English, Copyright 1996 by the International Reading Association and the National Council for Teachers of English. Reprinted with permission.

Information Literacy Standards for Student Learning

Information Literacy

Standard 1: The student who is information literate accesses information efficiently and effectively.

Standard 2: The student who is information literate evaluates information critically and competently.

Standard 3: The student who is information literate uses information accurately and creatively.

Independent Learning

Standard 4: The student who is an independent learner is information literate and pursues information related to personal interests.

Standard 5: The student who is an independent learner is information literate and appreciates literature and other creative expressions of information.

Standard 6: The student who is an independent learner is information literate and strives for excellence in information seeking and knowledge generation.

Social Responsibility

Standard 7: The student who contributes positively to the learning community and to society is information literate and recognizes the importance of information to a democratic society.

Standard 8: The student who contributes positively to the learning community and to society is information literate and practices ethical behavior in regard to information and information technology.

Standard 9: The student who contributes positively to the learning community and to society is information literate and participates effectively in groups to pursue and generate information.

The American Library Association and the Association for Educational Communications and Technology. Copyright 1998. Reprinted with permission from the American Library Association.

The Standards Alignment Chart found in Figure SC1 helps teachers and librarians align their instruction with the Information Literacy Standards for Student Learning and the NCTE/IRA Standards for the English Language Arts. This chart includes the number of the standard(s) addressed in each lesson within each chapter.

Figure SC1: Standards Alignment Chart

TITLE OF SELECTION	AME OF ACTIVITY	INFORMATION LITERACY STANDARDS FOR STUDENT LEARNING	NCTE/IRA STANDARDS FOR THE ENGLISH LANGUAGE ARTS
I Never Had It Made: The Autobiography of Jackie Robinson	Research and Writing	1, 2, 3, 4, 6, 7, 8 ,9	1, 3, 5, 6, 11, 12
	Sports Reporting	1, 2, 3, 4, 6, 7, 8, 9	1, 3, 5, 6, 11, 12
	Questions to Guide Your Reading	1, 2, 3, 4, 9	1, 2, 4, 6, 7, 9, 10, 11, 12
	Quotable Quotes	1, 3, 4, 11, 12	1, 2, 3, 4
	Creating a Mural	1, 2, 3, 4	1, 3, 5, 11, 12
	Creating a Postage Stamp	1, 2, 3, 4, 6, 8, 9	1, 3, 4, 5, 7, 8, 10, 11, 12
	Hero Writing	1, 2, 3, 4, 5, 6, 7, 8, 9	3, 4, 5, 6, 7, 10, 11, 12
The Young Landlords	Activating Prior Knowledge	1, 2, 3, 4, 9	1, 3, 4, 5, 10, 11, 12
	Setting a Purpose for Reading	1, 2, 3, 6, 7, 8, 9	1, 3, 4, 10, 11, 12
	Slang Log	1, 2, 3, 4, 7	1, 3, 4, 5, 6, 9, 10, 11, 12
	Point of View Writing/ Business Letter	1, 2, 3, 4, 9	1, 2, 4, 6, 7, 9, 10, 11, 12
	Budgeting for Renovations	1, 2, 3, 4, 6, 7, 8, 9	1, 3, 4, 5, 6, 7, 8, 10, 11, 12
	Service Learning/ Solving Problems	1, 2, 3, 4, 6, 7, 8, 9	1, 3, 4, 5, 6, 7, 8, 10, 11, 12
	Neighborhood Picture Books	1, 2, 3, 4, 6, 7, 8, 9	1, 3, 4, 5, 6, 7, 8, 10, 11, 12
Everett Anderson's Goodbye	Picture Walk Reaction	1, 7	4, 11, 12
	Illustration Interpretation	3, 9	1, 11, 12
	Writing your Feelings	1, 3, 5, 9	1, 3, 4, 9, 10, 11, 12
	Drawing your Feelings	1, 3, 5, 9	1, 3, 4, 9, 10, 11, 12
	Writing for Impact/Haiku Writing	1, 3, 4, 5, 9	1, 3, 4, 5, 6, 9, 10, 11, 12
	Becoming a Children's Book Author	1, 2, 3, 4, 5, 9	1, 2, 3, 4, 5, 6, 7, 8, 9, 10, 11, 12
The People Could Fly: American Black Folktales	Spirituals	1, 2, 3, 4, 5, 6, 7, 8, 9	1, 2, 3, 4, 5, 6, 7, 8, 9, 10, 11, 12
	Timeline	1, 2, 3, 4, 5, 6, 7, 8, 9	1, 2, 3, 4, 5, 6, 7, 8, 9, 10, 11, 12
	Discussion Questions/ Journal Writing	1, 2, 3, 4, 9	1, 2, 4, 6, 9, 10, 11, 12
	The Award Goes To …	1, 2, 3, 4, 5, 6, 7, 8, 9	1, 2, 3, 4, 5, 6, 9, 10, 11, 12
	Writing a Folktale	1, 2, 3, 4, 5, 6, 7, 8, 9	1, 2, 3, 4, 5, 6, 9, 10, 11, 12
	Exploring Slave Narratives through Diary Writing	1, 2, 3, 4, 5, 6, 7, 8, 9	1, 2, 3, 4, 5, 6, 9, 10, 11, 12
	Readers Theatre	1, 2, 3, 4, 5, 6, 7, 8, 9	1, 2, 3, 4, 5, 6, 9, 10, 11, 12
Justin and the Best Biscuits in the World	Research Writing	1, 2, 3, 4, 6, 7, 8, 9	1, 3, 4, 5, 6, 7, 8, 10, 11, 12
	Family Tree	1, 2, 3, 4, 6, 7, 8, 9	1, 3, 4, 5, 6, 7, 8, 10, 11, 12
	Questions to Guide Reading	1, 2, 3, 4, 9	1, 2, 4, 6, 9, 11, 12
	Similes	1, 2, 3, 6	1, 3, 4, 5, 6, 11, 12
	Scrapbooking	1, 2, 3	1, 3, 4, 5, 6, 8, 9, 11, 12
	Literal vs. Inferential Meanings	1, 2	1, 3, 4, 5, 6, 11, 12
	Comparison Using a Venn diagram	1, 2, 3	1, 3, 4, 5, 6, 11, 12
	Women's Work/Men's Work	1, 2, 3	1, 3, 4, 5, 6, 11, 12

	Creating a Festival Poster	1, 2, 3, 6	1, 3, 4, 5, 6, 7, 8, 11, 12
	Creating a Dust Cover	1, 2, 3, 6	1, 3, 4, 5, 6, 7, 8, 11, 12
Fallen Angels	KWL/Vietnam Research	1, 2, 3, 4, 6, 7, 8, 9	1, 3, 5, 6, 11, 12
	Vocabulary Notebook	1, 2, 3, 6, 9	1, 3, 9, 11, 12
	Character Study	1, 2, 3, 9	1, 3, 5, 9, 11, 12
	Photo Quotes	1, 2, 3, 4, 6, 7, 8, 9	1, 3, 4, 5, 6, 7, 8, 11, 12
	Letters Home	1, 2, 3, 4, 6, 7, 8, 9	1, 3, 5, 6, 11, 12
	War Memorial	1, 2, 3, 6, 7, 8, 9	1, 2, 3, 4, 5, 7, 8, 11, 12
	Media Coverage	1, 2, 3, 4, 6, 7, 8, 9	1, 3, 5, 6, 11, 12
	Guest Speaker	7, 8, 9	4, 7, 11, 12
	Discussion Questions/ Essay Questions	1, 2, 3	1, 3, 4, 5, 6, 8, 11, 12
The Road to Memphis	Family Discussion	1, 2, 3, 4, 6, 7, 8, 9	1, 3, 5, 6, 11, 12
	Vocabulary Term Tracker	1, 2, 3, 4, 6	1, 3, 4, 5, 6, 11, 12
	Role Play: Mississippi 1941	1, 2, 3, 4, 5, 6, 7, 8, 9	1, 3, 5, 6, 11, 12
	Class Discussion Questions/Writing Prompts	1, 2, 3, 4, 6, 7, 8, 9	1, 3, 5, 6, 9, 11, 12
	Question Answer Relationships		
	Chapter Mapping		
	Author Information Brochure/Booktalk		
Toning the Sweep	Journaling Writing	1, 2, 3, 4, 9	1, 2, 4, 6, 9, 10, 11, 12
	Tragedy Exercise	3	3, 4, 9, 11, 12
	Desert Anticipation Guide	1, 2, 3, 4, 5, 6, 7, 8, 9	1, 3, 4, 5, 6, 8, 11, 12
	Alabama in 1964	1, 2, 3	1, 3, 4, 5, 6, 8, 11, 12
	Personal History: A Visual Representation	1, 2, 3	1, 3, 4, 5, 6, 8, 11, 12
	Biography Study	1, 2, 3, 4, 5, 6	1, 3, 4, 5, 6, 8, 11, 12
	Writing Prompts	1, 2, 3, 4, 9	1, 2, 4, 6, 9, 10, 11, 12
Slam!	Prior to Reading Discussion	1, 9	4, 9, 11, 12
	Dream Job Research	1, 2, 3, 9	1, 3, 4, 5, 6, 7, 8, 11, 12
	Tour of Harlem	1, 2, 3, 9	1, 3, 4, 5, 6, 7, 8, 11, 12
	Literature Circles	1, 2, 3, 5, 9	1, 2, 3, 4, 5, 6, 9, 10, 11, 12
	Character Change	1, 2, 3, 9	1, 3, 4, 9, 10, 11, 12
	Discussion Questions	1, 9	4, 9, 11, 12
	Writing an Afterward	4, 5, 6	1, 3, 4, 5, 6, 9, 11, 12
	Book Review	1, 2, 3, 4, 5, 6, 8, 9	1, 3, 4, 5, 6, 9, 11, 12
	Annotations Compilation	1, 2, 3, 4, 5, 6, 7, 8, 9	1, 3, 4, 5, 6, 9, 11, 12
Heaven	Questions to Ponder	1, 2, 3, 4, 9	1, 2, 4, 6, 9, 10, 11, 12
	Comparing Three Sources/ The 1963 Birmingham Bombing	1, 2, 3, 4, 5, 6, 7, 8, 9	1, 2, 3, 4, 5, 6, 7, 8, 9, 11, 12
	Researching Names	1, 7, 8, 9	1, 3, 5, 6, 8, 11, 12
	Dream Detectives	1, 7, 8, 9	1, 3, 7, 8, 9, 11, 12
	Timely Music	1, 4, 9	11, 12
	Writing to Relatives	1, 2, 3, 4, 5, 6	1, 2, 3, 4, 5, 9, 11, 12
	Secrets	1, 9	11, 12
	Comic Strip	1, 9	4, 9, 11, 12

The First Part Last	Parent Interview	1, 3	4, 7, 11, 12
	Class Discussion Questions	1, 2, 3, 4, 9	1, 2, 4, 6, 9, 10, 11, 12
	Finding Conflict	1, 2	1, 3, 4, 5, 6, 11, 12
	Making a Connection/ Class Chain Link	1, 2	1, 3, 4, 5, 6, 11, 12
	Vocabulary Word Bank	1, 2	1, 3, 4, 5, 6, 11, 12
	Database	1, 2, 3, 6, 7, 8, 9	1, 3, 4, 5, 6, 11, 12
	Writing an Editorial	3, 5	1, 3, 4, 5, 6, 11, 12
	Writing a Script	3, 5	1, 3, 4, 5, 6, 11, 12
	Slave Research	1, 2, 3, 5, 6, 7, 8, 9	1, 3, 4, 5, 6, 11, 12
	Emancipation Proclamation/Slavery	1, 2, 3, 5, 6, 7, 8, 9	1, 3, 4, 5, 6, 11, 12
	Family Ties	1, 2, 3	1, 3, 4, 5, 6, 11, 12
Copper Sun	Writing Prompts/ Discussion Questions	1, 2, 3, 4, 9	1, 2, 4, 6, 9, 10, 11, 12
	Character List	3	1, 3, 4, 5, 6, 11, 12
	Point of View Correspondence	3, 5	1, 3, 4, 5, 6, 11, 12
	Slave Journals	3, 5	1, 3, 4, 5, 6, 11, 12
	Visual Representation	3, 5	1, 3, 4, 5, 6, 11, 12
	Amari's Timeline	3, 5	1, 3, 4, 5, 6, 11, 12

PART 1

Award-Winning
Book Selections

CHAPTER 1

I Never Had It Made: The Autobiography of Jackie Robinson

Bibliographic Information

Title: *I Never Had It Made: The Autobiography of Jackie Robinson*

Author(s): Jackie Robinson, as told to Alfred Duckett

Copyright: 1972

Publisher: Putnam

1973 Coretta Scott King Award Winner

Annotation

This book chronicles the accomplishments and struggles of baseball great, Jackie Robinson. This autobiography is not just about baseball: it is about the breaking of the color barrier in American baseball, and it is about a man's desire to achieve justice for himself and all Americans. Sports readers will find themselves involved in the turmoil Robinson faced when, in 1947, he joined the Brooklyn Dodgers as the first black baseball player. The story of triumph, cultural heroism, and American history is sure to be one that is enjoyed in both adult and young adult collections.

Grade Level: grade 9 and up   **ISBN:** 0880014199

Discussion Starters/Writing Prompts/Pre-Reading Activities

Research and Writing

Information Literacy Standards for Student Learning: 1, 2, 3, 4, 6, 7, 8, 9

NCTE/IRA Standards for the English Language Arts: 1, 3, 5, 6, 11, 12

Prior to reading the text, require students to begin completion of the KWLQ chart as they investigate the history of the Negro Baseball League and the status of the United States in 1947 on the Internet or using other sources. The KWLQ chart is available for reproduction in Figure 1.1. The students complete the first column with any background information or prior knowledge they possess about the Negro Baseball League; column two requires students to compile a list of information they want to learn from the text; column three is completed after the research is conducted. This column requires students to make a list of things that they learned; column four requires students to write any questions they still have about the topic. The Web site <http://www.negroleaguebaseball.com/> is a good place for students to begin their online search of information. Then, ask students to answer the following questions in their reflective journal and be prepared to discuss.

1. Why was Jackie Robinson's recruitment by the Brooklyn Dodgers so important in 1947?

2. What was happening in 1947 that would make it so important?

3. If you were Jackie Robinson, would you have made the same choice? Why or why not?

4. Based on what was happening in the United States, what might you have done differently?

5. Generate a definition of a hero. Who is your hero? Why?

The KWLQ can be used as an assessment tool by reviewing what students learned and listed in the third column. The last column, Q, is a great means for informing future instruction on this particular topic. Finally, make a class KWLQ chart and hang it on the wall and allow students to add information learned from research and other sources as information arises.

Collaboration between classroom teachers and librarians will enhance this lesson tremendously. Classroom teachers should ask the librarian for additional resources for this activity. Students are informally assessed on the completion of the KWLQ and the answers to writing prompts.

Figure 1.1: KWLQ

K	W	L	Q
What We Think We KNOW	**What We WANT to Find Out**	**What We LEARNED**	**What Other QUESTIONS Do We Have?**

Sports Reporting

Information Literacy Standards for Student Learning: 1, 2, 3, 4, 6, 7, 8, 9

NCTE/IRA Standards for the English Language Arts: 1, 3, 5, 6, 11, 12

Have students research the baseball career of Jackie Robinson and write an article for a newspaper sports page. Students can use information gathered from multiple sources: interviews, Internet, books, and articles to generate facts for their articles. Before beginning to write, require students to complete the 5 W's Graphic Organizer in Figure 1.2. Use this organizer as a prewriting activity to help students generate and organize ideas. The lead of a newspaper article contains the 5 W's (Who? What? Where? When? Why?) and these questions can be used to write the first paragraph of the article. After completing the graphic organizer and developing a lead paragraph, allow students to write a rough draft of their article. After they write rough drafts, assign students to be "peer" editors and "peer" fact checkers for articles. Then have them write a final draft using a word processing program on the computer. When articles are complete, create a sports page for 1947 using a publishing program. After reading the book, students may want to revise their articles to include other facts about Robinson's life that they learned during their reading. Soon, students will realize that Robinson was not just a man of baseball, but a man of character and great achievements. Create a final sports page for distribution in the school library or school-wide. Articles can be assessed using the Sports Reporting Rubric found in Figure 1.3. As an alternative, students can create their article using a Web 2.0 resource found at <http://cogdogroo.wikispaces.com/StoryTools>.

Figure 1.2: 5 W's Graphic Organizer

Name: _____ **Date:** _____

Topic: _____

What?	
Who?	
Why?	
When?	
Where?	

Figure 1.3: Sports Reporting Rubric

CRITERIA	EXCELLENT (5)	GOOD (4)	AVERAGE (3)	BELOW AVERAGE (2)	POOR (1)
Prewriting	Student used the 5 W's graphic organizer during the prewriting stage to generate ideas for the article.				Student did not use the 5 W's graphic organizer during the prewriting stage to generate ideas for the article.
Lead	Lead was extremely well-written, grabbed the reader's attention, and included the 5 W's.	Lead was well-written, grabbed the reader's attention and included the 5 W's.	Lead was satisfactory. It either did not grab the reader's attention or did not include all of the 5 W's.	Student did not use the 5 W's graphic organizer during the prewriting stage to generate ideas for the article.	Lead was not well-written because it did not grab the reader's attention and did not include the 5 W's.
Body of Article	The body of the article was extremely well written. It grasped the main information, listed the information in order of importance, and was written in third person.	The body of the article was well written. It grasped the main information, listed the information in order of importance, and was written in third person.	The body of the article was satisfactory. It either did not grasp the main information, OR list the information in order of importance, OR was not written in third person.	Lead was written in a way that either did not grab the reader's attention or did not include the 5 W's. The body of the article was written in a way that did not grasp the main information, was not listed in order of importance, and was not written in third person.	The body of the article did not meet the requirements of the assignment.
Mechanics	There are 0-1 errors in capitalization, punctuation, and/or grammar.	There are 2-3 errors in capitalization, punctuation, and/or grammar.	There are 4-5 errors in capitalization, punctuation, and/or grammar.	There are 6-7 errors in capitalization, punctuation, and/or grammar.	There are 8 or more errors in capitalization, punctuation, and/or grammar.

Literary Strategies for During Reading

Questions to Guide Your Reading

Information Literacy Standards for Student Learning: 1, 2, 3, 4, 9

NCTE/IRA Standards for the English Language Arts: 1, 2, 4, 6, 7, 9, 10, 11, 12

Use the following list of discussion prompts while reading the text. These questions can be used as writing prompts also.

1. Discuss the obstacles that Jackie Robinson faced before baseball, during baseball, and after baseball.

2. Discuss why Jackie Robinson is considered such a great man. What qualities did he have that make him so?

3. Discuss Jackie Robinson's involvement with the Civil Rights Movement. What impact did his voice provide for the cause?

4. Discuss Jackie Robinson's unforgettable breaking of the color barrier with the Dodgers. How might you feel if you were him? What would you have done the same? Differently?

Quotable Quotes

Information Literacy Standards for Student Learning: 1, 2, 3, 4

NCTE/IRA Standards for the English Language Arts: 1, 3, 4, 11, 12

Many of Jackie Robinson's quotes have multiple meanings. While reading the text, periodically share with students one of Robinson's quotes listed below. Display the quote on the bulletin board or chalkboard and invite students to write their interpretation of the quote or ask them to write how the quote may or may not relate to their own lives. Students may begin to notice that Robinson was not just a baseball player but a man of character and wisdom. Challenge students to keep a "Quote Book." When students find interesting or intriguing quotes either in reading or conversation, they can write the quote in their "Quote Book." Students can then display their own quotes for peer interpretation. The following is a list of some of Robinson's quotes:

- "Baseball is like a poker game. Nobody wants to quit when he's losing, nobody wants you to quit when you're ahead."
- "A life is not important except in the impact it has on other lives."
- "I'm not concerned with your liking or disliking me . . . all I ask is that you respect me as a human being."
- "There's not an American in this country free until every one of us is free."
- "The right of every American to first-class citizenship is the most important issue of our time."
- "Life is not a spectator sport. If you're going to spend your whole life in the grand-stand just watching what is going on, in my opinion you're wasting your life."

Whole class or small group discussion will ensure students successfully understood and interpreted the quotes. Essentially students should relate the quote to their own lives in some way.

Post-Reading Activities

Creating a Mural

Information Literacy Standards for Student Learning: 1, 2, 3, 4

NCTE/IRA Standards for the English Language Arts: 1, 3, 4, 5, 11, 12

For this activity, have students choose an image that represents their reaction to the book. Using butcher paper, allow students to create a class mural that represents their reactions and interpretations of the book. Students can use paints, pencils, charcoal or crayons, depending on their preference. Display the mural in the library or hallway for spectators to enjoy. For students who do not consider themselves artists, invite them to use words instead of images to convey their unique message. All students should be actively involved in the creation of the mural.

Creating a Postage Stamp

Information Literacy Standards for Student Learning: 1, 2, 3, 4, 6, 8, 9

NCTE/IRA Standards for the English Language Arts: 1, 3, 4, 5, 7, 8, 10, 11, 12

The United States Post Office displays many prominent Americans on postage stamps. Ask students to create a postage stamp in honor of Jackie Robinson. Students can draw the images or create the images on the computer. Encourage students to work collaboratively in small groups to complete this project. Students can view past and present postage stamps prior to the assignment. Each postage stamp should include a title, design, and image. It should also incorporate technology or other media. As a final requirement, each postage stamp should include facts or new information. Students can view postal stamps at the U.S. Postal service Web site at <www.usps.com>. If requiring students to work collaboratively, the Collaboration Checksheet in Figure 1.4 will help students self-evaluate their performance. Additionally, the Postage Stamp Rubric in Figure 1.5 can be used to evaluate each student or group project. Display postage stamps in the hallway or on a bulletin board. Require students to write a one- to two-page reflective narrative about the role they played in the creation of the postage stamp if cooperative learning was utilized.

Figure 1.4: Collaboration Checksheet

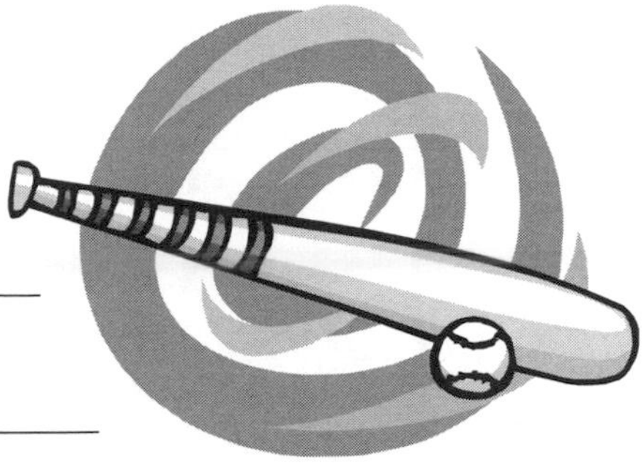

Group Member: _____

Other Group Members: _____

Answer each question honestly as you evaluate your own contributions to the group project.

Task	Strong	Okay	Weak
I contributed fully and equally to this project.			
I worked more than the other members of the group.			
I contributed ideas.			
I helped write the assignment.			
I helped revise and edit the assignment when appropriate.			
I helped in the production of the project.			
I performed tasks that were not asked of me.			
I met with members of my group outside of class or library time.			

Figure 1.5: Postage Stamp Rubric

Name(s): _____

Criteria	Excellent (3)	Average (2)	Poor (1)
	Contains all required elements including a title, design, and image.	Missing two of the three required.	Missing three of the three required.
	Exemplary presentation and use of technology or other media. It is apparent that much time and effort was spent on this assignment.	Average presentation. Does not use appropriate technology or other media.	Sloppy presentation. Not final draft quality. Does not use appropriate technology or other media.
	Includes many facts and new information interesting to the sender (reader).	Includes some facts or new information interesting to the sender (reader).	Does not include facts or new information interesting to the sender (reader).

Hero Writing

Information Literacy Standards for Student Learning: 3, 4, 5, 6, 7, 9

NCTE/IRA Standards for the English Language Arts: 1, 2, 3, 4, 5, 6, 7, 8, 9, 10, 11, 12

Robinson was a hero to many Americans. Ask students to write a narrative paper about their personal hero and type it using a word processing program. Students' heroes may be famous personalities, a family member, or friend. Ask students to include a detailed description of why the person is their hero. Prior to writing, ask students to brainstorm the criteria for being a hero and use this information as a guide for the selection of their heroes. Encourage students to include a picture with their paper. If the person is still living, ask students to send a copy of the paper to the person so they know they are appreciated and respected. Students may be surprised at the reactions they receive in return. Use the Hero Writing Assignment Rubric in Figure 1.6 as an assessment tool for this writing assignment.

Figure 1.6: Hero Writing Rubric Levels of Performance

PERFORMANCE INDICATORS	OUTSTANDING (10)	COMPETENT (8)	SATISFACTORY (6)	POOR (4)	UNACCEPTABLE (1)
Word Choice	Writer uses vivid adjectives and/or phrases that draw pictures in the reader's mind. The placement of words is precise.	Writer uses vivid adjectives and/or phrases that draw pictures in the reader's mind. The placement of words is not always accurate.	Writer uses adjectives and/or phrases but the choice of words lacks variety. Placement of words is not always accurate.	Writer uses a limited vocabulary and does not draw pictures in the reader's mind and/or interest.	Writer uses a limited and inappropriate vocabulary and does not draw pictures in the reader's mind and/or interest. Word choice is distracting to the reader.
Sentence structure	All sentences are well-constructed and varied in length and structure. Sentence fluency is mastered.	Most sentences are well-constructed and varied in length and structure.	Most sentences are well-constructed but have similar length and structure.	Sentences lack structure and have similar length and structure.	Sentences lack structure and many are incomplete.
Mechanics	No errors in grammar, spelling or mechanics present.	1-2 errors in grammar, spelling or mechanics present.	3-4 errors in grammar, spelling or mechanics present.	5-6 errors in grammar, spelling or mechanics present.	7-8 errors in grammar, spelling or mechanics present.
Focus	There is one clear, well-written focused topic present in paper. Main ideas are supported with details in a thorough and complete manner	Main idea of the paper is clear but the supporting information in general in nature and does not fully support the main idea.	Main idea is somewhat clear but more supporting details are needed.		Main idea is unclear. Supporting details are lacking.

Additional Information about the Author

Both Jackie Robinson and Alfred Duckett are credited with writing this story. Much of the information was told to Alfred Duckett, a freelance writer, by Jackie Robinson. Duckett co-authored another book with Robinson titled *Breakthrough to the Big League, the Story of Jackie Robinson* published in 1965 by Harper and Row. Duckett is probably best known by his collaborative efforts with Dr. Martin Luther King, Jr. on a book and speeches, including Dr. King's "I Have a Dream" speech for the 1963 March on Washington. Mr. Duckett also assisted Dr. King in the writing of both "Why We Can't Wait," a book on the civil rights movement, and "My Dream," a syndicated newspaper column. He died in 1984 at the age of 67.

Additional Resource

Electronic Resources

The National Archives. *Teaching with Documents: Beyond the Playing Field—Jackie Robinson, Civil Rights Advocate*. 28 April 2008 <http://www.archives.gov/education/lessons/Jackie-robinson/>

This National Archives sponsored Web site provides resources for teachers and librarians to teach many different eras from U.S. history. Lesson plans, assessment tools, and standards correlations are provided.

Schwartz, L. (2007). *Jackie Changed Face of Sports*. Retrieved April 28, 2008 from <http://espn.go.com/sportscentury/features/00016431.html>.

This article chronicles Jackie Robinson's sports career by providing readers with a timeline of his successes and obstacles both in his professional and personal life.

Howard, P. (2003, May 15). *The Official Site of Jackie Robinson*. Retrieved April 28, 2008 from <http://www.jackierobinson.com>.

The official site includes a biography, baseball statistics, photographs, achievements, quotes, and much more relating to Jackie Robinson. This is a prime place to begin research on Jackie Robinson.

National Baseball Hall of Fame, Inc. (2008). *Baseball Hall of Fame*. Retrieved October, 21, 2008 from <http://web.baseballhalloffame.org/index.jsp>.

This is the Web site of the National Baseball Hall of Fame. Students can learn about the many educational services offered or visit the "Sights and Sounds" section and watch videos. This Web site offers many opportunities for students to learn about Jackie Robinson and other historical sports figures.

Major League Baseball Advanced Media (2008). Retrieved October 21, 2008 from <http://mlb.mlb.com/index.jsp>.

Sponsored by Major League Baseball, this Web site contains everything related to Jackie Robinson that students might be interested in researching: career timelines, batting averages, speeches, and quotes. It also includes information about

Breaking Barriers: In Sports, In Life, which is a national character education program sponsored by Major League Baseball and written by Jackie Robinson's daughter, Sharon Robinson.

Books

Dorinson, J. & Wamund, J. (1999). *Robinson: Race, Sports, and the American Dream.* New York: M.E. Sharpe.

This book chronicles a Long Island University's three-day celebration of the day Robinson became the first African American to play major league baseball. This book includes presentations from people who attended and participated in that celebration, especially chosen for their unique insights into the life of Jackie Robinson. President Bill Clinton was just one of the prominent figures that contributed to this exciting and monumental event.

Rampersad, A. (1998). *Jackie Robinson: A Biography.* New York: Ballantine Books.

A comprehensive biography of Jackie Robinson that was written by a Princeton professor and author.

Robinson, S. (2002). *Jackie's Nine: Jackie Robinson's Value to Live By.* New York: Scholastic.

This book, written by Jackie Robinson's daughter, portrays the life and values of Jackie Robinson. In each chapter, Ms. Robinson describes the challenges that she and her family faced throughout their lives. Ms. Robinson describes to the reader her father's values exemplifying courage, determination, teamwork, persistence and commitment, to name a few.

Robinson, S. (2004). *Promises to Keep: How Jackie Robinson Changed America.* New York: Scholastic.

Sharon Robinson chronicles the life of her father. Intended for grades 4 to 7.

CHAPTER 2

The Young Landlords

Bibliographic Information

Title: *The Young Landlords*

Author(s): Walter Dean Myers

Copyright: 1979

Publisher: Peter Smith

1980 Coretta Scott King Award Winner

Annotation

Fifteen-year old Paul Williams is involved in the creation of an "action group" in his Harlem neighborhood. Hoping to fill their summer with excitement, Paul and his friends find themselves landlords of a slum when they purchase a building for one dollar. Paul and his friends quickly realize that with tenants come problems. One problem after another consumes the teen landlords' summer vacation. The summer adventure proves to be a challenge, but a challenge well-worth the effort.

Grade Level: grade 4 and up   **ISBN:** 0140342443

Discussion Starters/Writing Prompts/Pre-Reading Activities

Activating Prior Knowledge

Information Literacy Standards for Student Learning: 1, 2, 3, 4, 9

NCTE/IRA Standards for the English Language Arts: 1, 3, 4, 5, 10, 11, 12

Create a class word web/cluster of the word *slang* on a large area of the wall or bulletin board. Encourage students to think about what the word means and provide examples and situations in which slang is appropriate or inappropriate to use in conversations. Discuss slang terms that students know and use daily in their own lives. Ask students to share examples. Allow students to write their slang terms on sentence strips and hang on the wall or bulletin board. The word web should be used as an ongoing word wall with additions made throughout the reading. When students read a slang term, allow them to include it on the word wall. A discussion of appropriate uses for slang terms is necessary for students to understand there is a time and place that slang use is acceptable, for instance, with friends. Choose one or two pages of the text that includes slang terms and read it aloud to the class. Furthermore, ask students to determine why they think Walter Dean Myers used so many slang terms in his writing. Ask students, "Does the use of slang bring the characters to life? Why or why not?" and "Does the use of slang terms make the text more authentic or believable? State examples from the text." Encourage students to create a modern-day slang dictionary containing definitions of slang terms, both old and new. Challenge students to interview parents and grandparents for generational slang terms for which today's teens are not familiar. Share dictionaries in class or designate a special shelf in the library to house the dictionaries.

Setting a Purpose for Reading

Information Literacy Standards for Student Learning: 1, 2, 3, 6, 7, 8, 9

NCTE/IRA Standards for the English Language Arts: 1, 3, 4, 10, 11, 12

Before reading the text, discuss the term *landlord* with students. Allow students to define this term in their own words. Next, require students to make predictions about the story. Ask students the following questions to set a purpose for their reading.

1. What is a landlord?

2. What are some responsibilities of a landlord?

3. Do you think teenagers could be landlords? Why or why not?

4. What do you think the story is about based on the title and cover of the book?

Literacy Strategies for During Reading

Slang Log

Information Literacy Standards for Student Learning: 1, 2, 3, 4, 7

NCTE/IRA Standards for the English Language Arts: 1, 3, 4, 5, 6, 9, 10, 11, 12

Give each student an 8½" x 11" sheet of paper and have them make four columns. Column one should be titled "Slang Term." Column two should be titled "Page Number and Context." Column three should be titled "Definition from Context," and column four should be titled "Dictionary or Friend." Have students keep an ongoing log of the slang terms they find while reading the text. Each time students find a term, ask them to write the term in column one under the heading "Slang Term." Then, have students write the page number and the sentence(s) in which the word was used in column two under "Page Number and Context." Next, have students use the context clues from the text to figure out the definition in their own words. This definition is written in column three under "Definition in Context." Finally, have students check their definition either in the dictionary, if appropriate, or ask a family member or friend for their interpretation. The "Slang Log" terms can be added to the word wall when time permits. Librarians or classroom teachers can informally assess students' comprehension of these terms and monitor their use of context clues. These terms can be added to the slang word wall created prior to reading.

Post-Reading Activities

Point of View Writing/Business Letter

Information Literacy Standards for Student Learning: 1, 2, 3, 4, 9

NCTE/IRA Standards for the English Language Arts: 1, 2, 4, 6, 7, 9, 10, 11, 12

Have students write a business letter from a tenant's point of view. Before writing, introduce students to the elements of a standard business letter: letterhead (or heading with a typed name, address and phone number), date, inside address, salutation with proper punctuation (colons :), body (text), complimentary closing with proper punctuation (a comma ,), signature, and a typed name. Encourage students to be as direct as possible in their letters, and they must support their complaints with facts. The letter should be typed using a word processing program on the computer. Use the Business Letter Rubric in Figure 2.1 for assessment purposes. Encourage students to share their letters with the class. As an extension activity, students can write a business letter to a company of personal interest. Students brainstorm reasons for writing a business letter of their own such as to complain about a service or product or provide praise about an employee. Addresses and contact information can be found on the Internet.

Figure 2.1: Business Letter Rubric

Components	High Quality (3)	Acceptable (2)	Needs Attention (1)	Possible	Actual
Return Address and Date	Return address is complete and accurate. Date in correct position. No errors in spelling and/or mechanics.	Return address is complete and accurate. Date in correct position. 1-2 errors in spelling and/or mechanics.	Return address is complete and accurate. Date in correct position. 3 or more errors in spelling and/or mechanics.	3	
Inside Address and Salutation	Inside address and salutation is complete and accurate. No errors in spelling and/or mechanics.	Inside address and salutation is complete and accurate. 1-2 errors in spelling and/or mechanics.	Inside address and salutation is complete and accurate. 3 or more errors in spelling and/or mechanics.	3	
Content	Message is complete and appropriate. Paragraph(s) are organized, logical, and sequential.	Message is somewhat complete. Paragraphs are somewhat organized, logical, and/or sequential.	Message is incomplete and/or the paragraphs are not logical, organized, and/or sequential.	3	
Closing, Signature	Closing is appropriate with written and typed signatures. Reference initials and enclosure are included, if necessary.	Missing one element in closing and/or signature.	Missing two or more elements in closing and/or signature.	3	
Mechanics	Letter has 0 errors in spelling, capitalization, punctuation, sentence structure, paragraphing, and/or subject-verb agreement.	Letter has 1-2 errors in spelling, capitalization, punctuation, sentence structure, paragraphing, and/or subject-verb agreement.	Letter has 3-4 errors in spelling, capitalization, punctuation, sentence structure, paragraphing, and/or subject-verb agreement.	3	

Budgeting for Renovations

Information Literacy Standards for Student Learning: 1, 2, 3, 4, 6, 7, 8, 9

NCTE/IRA Standards for the English Language Arts: 1, 3, 4, 5, 6, 7, 8, 10, 11, 12

Although improving the appearance of a home or apartment building sounds inviting, the cost can be tremendously expensive. To teach students the realities of renovations, have students work in small groups to plan a renovation of a kitchen. Set a limited budget, for instance $10,000. This may seem like a lot of money until students begin working on their new kitchen. Allow students to use the Internet, newspaper, or other print media to research products and prices. Then, students can use a spreadsheet to keep track of their expenditures. Any spreadsheet computer program can be used for this assignment. Students can use the following Web sites to begin their renovation research:

* <www.homedepot.com>
* <www.lowes.com>
* <www.doitbest.com>
* <www.acehardware.com>
* <www.amazon.com>

After each group completes their research and budget spreadsheet, require groups to write a reflective one-page summary of their experience. Questions to prompt their writing might include: What was challenging about this project? What surprised you? Did you make predictions that came true? What did you learn from this assignment? By reading students' reflective papers, the librarian or classroom teacher can determine if students understand the amount of time and money involved in renovating one room in a home. Finally, encourage groups to share their expenditures and compare their costs to the costs of other groups, as well as their experience.

Service Learning/Solving Problems

Information Literacy Standards for Student Learning: 1, 2, 3, 4, 6, 7, 8, 9

NCTE/IRA Standards for the English Language Arts: 1, 3, 4, 5, 6, 7, 8, 10, 11, 12

The Action Group in *The Young Landlords* intends to solve a community problem. Ask students to brainstorm a list of problems in their own community. What can they do to help with these problems? Decide, as a group, a problem they can solve in their own community. Plan a short-term plan for this problem. A long-term plan may evolve from the project as well. Encourage students to enlist help from classmates, teachers, parents, administrators, and community members.

Neighborhood Picture Books/Writing for a Younger Audience

Information Literacy Standards for Student Learning: 1, 2, 3, 4, 6, 7, 8, 9

NCTE/IRA Standards for the English Language Arts: 1, 3, 4, 5, 6, 7, 8, 10, 11, 12

Share the picture book *Harlem* by Walter Dean Myers. Explain to students that this Caldecott Honor book and Coretta Scott King Honor book was written by Walter Dean Myers and illustrated by his son, Christopher Myers. The text is a poem that expresses the spirit of Harlem in terms of art, music, literature, and other areas of life. Allow students to respond to the words and pictures, and then require students to work in groups to develop their own picture book about their neighborhood. Remind students that Myers was able to make this book come alive to the reader because he lived in Harlem and it is important to him. His own personal experience prompted him to write an eloquent text filled with colorful and vivid language. Students should consider using their own experiences to do the same. Likewise, students can relate to their own neighborhood and bring it to life for readers. Challenge students to illustrate the picture books as well. Students should include a well-developed setting, characters, and plot. Furthermore, students should pay special attention to the concept they are trying to develop as well as writing conventions. Provide the rubric for students prior to writing so they can use it to create their books. Once all picture books are completed, laminate the pages and bind for display in the library or donate to an elementary building or senior center. As an alternative, provide students with disposable cameras to take pictures of their community or neighborhood to make their words come to life. Use the Neighborhood Picture Book Rubric found in Figure 2.2 for assessment purposes.

Additional Information about the Author

Walter Dean Myers is a writer of countless children's and young adult literature selections. He was born in West Virginia in 1937 but spent most of his childhood and young adult life in Harlem. He was raised by foster parents and remembers a happy but tumultuous life while going through his own teen years.

Figure 2.2: Neighborhood Picture Book Rubric

Writer's Name(s):_____

	4	3	2	1
Setting	Detailed description of the setting including time and place that includes a vivid description so the reader can "see" the setting.	Somewhat detailed description of the setting including time and place.	Few details about the time or place. It is somewhat difficult to visualize the setting of the story.	Either the place or time is not evident in the story. No setting apparent. Characters are not developed.
Characters	Extremely well-developed characters. Actions, feeling, behaviors, appearance, and dialogue are detailed and appropriate for the text.	Somewhat well-developed characters. Actions, feeling, behaviors, appearance, and dialogue are detailed and appropriate for the text.	Few details about the characters are apparent. The characters are somewhat vague. Not much dialogue is used to bring the characters to life.	The reader knows very little about the characters from the text. No dialogue is included.
Plot	All plot elements are included in a well-organized and developed manner.	All plot elements are included in an organized and developed manner.	Two plot elements included but lack development.	More than two plot elements lack development.
Conventions	No errors in spelling, punctuation, or capitalization.	1-3 errors in spelling, punctuation, or capitalization.	4-6 errors in spelling, punctuation, or capitalization.	7-9 errors in spelling, punctuation, or capitalization.

Electronic Resources

African-American Literature Book Club. (2007). Retrieved July 22, 2008 from <http://aalbc.com/authors/walter1.htm>.

> This Web site provides information about Walter Dean Myers and other prominent African- American authors of interest. There are summaries of books by authors and interviews.

Walter Dean Myers (2008) Retrieved July 2, 2008 from <http://www.walterdeanmyers.net/bio.html>.

> This Web site of Walter Dean Myers includes a biography, news, contact information, and reviews. Fans of Walter Dean Myers will find background information on the author, father, and teacher. His latest public appearances are posted on the Web site, and users can contact the author directly via email through this Web site.

Current Books by Walter Dean Myers

Myers, W.D. (2008). *Sunrise over Fallujah.* New York: Scholastic.

> Myers brings the current Iraq War to life in another powerful novel. Against his father's wishes, Robin Perry chooses the military over going to college in 2003. He finds himself near the border of Iraq, struggling to understand who he is and what he is doing there. A current affairs lesson combined with drama that is sure to keep young adults intrigued and engaged.

Myers, W. D. (2007). *What They Found: Love on 145th Street.* New York: Wendy Lamb Books.

> The intertwining stories of teens from inner-city Harlem take on new life as the text is read. Each story stands alone, but some are connected, and readers familiar with Myers' *145th Street* (2000) will welcome back some familiar characters.

Myers, W.D. (2007). *Street Love.* New York: Amistad.

> The flow of these short poems carries readers along in thoughts, conversations, and scenes as Damien and Junice's romance unfolds. Damien, a high achiever who has been accepted to Brown University, is expected to be successful. Junice, who has just lost her mother to prison, is trying to keep her younger sister and her grandmother together as a family. This book is a perfect text for a readers theatre performance.

CHAPTER 3

Everett Anderson's Goodbye

Bibliographic Information

Title: *Everett Anderson's Goodbye*

Author(s): Lucille Clifton

Copyright: 1983

Publisher: The Trumpet Club

1984 Coretta Scott King Award Winner

Annotation

Lucille Clifton writes a short and poignant narrative of the stages of grief. The illustrations that accompany the text tell a provocative story that is appropriate for all ages when dealing with the death of a family member. This tough topic is appropriate for any student who may be struggling with this issue or knows someone who is struggling with this issue. Furthermore, by using this text with adolescents, they have the opportunity to display compassion and empathy for others; lessons often missing from the traditional content curriculum.

Grade Level: ages 5-8; interest level: all ages   **ISBN:** 9780805008005

Discussion Starters/Writing Prompts/Pre-Reading Activities

Picture Walk Reaction

Information Literacy Standards for Student Learning: 1, 7

NCTE/IRA Standards for the English Language Arts: 4, 11, 12

Conduct a picture walk with students choosing illustrations that tell the story. Do not read the text to students at this point. After showing each illustration, ask students to predict what story the text will tell. Make a class list of predictions on the board. Show each page slowly and prompt students to revise their predictions. Take class time to allow students to revise their predictions so they have a strong sense of setting a purpose for reading. Next, review the table of contents that lists the five stages of grief. Take time to discuss each stage and provide an example of each. The stages of grief include denial, anger, bargaining, depression, and acceptance. Invite students to share their own stories of grief if they feel comfortable doing so. Emphasize that a text with few words can portray an important message.

Literacy Strategies for During Reading

Illustration Interpretation

Information Literacy Standards for Student Learning: 1, 2, 3, 4, 7

NCTE/IRA Standards for the English Language Arts: 1, 3, 4, 5, 6, 9, 10, 11, 12

Although this text is a picture book, the text and illustrations can help readers of all ages who have lost a loved one. The author, Lucille Clifton, takes the reader through the stages of grief with few words but poignant illustrations. Read the text without showing the illustrations (after the picture walk). Once the librarian or classroom teacher reads the words on each page, ask students to conduct a quick draw on a blank piece of paper noting the page number. Have students use images to depict what the words have spoken. This will provide students with an opportunity to explore and relate to the words. This is done best with a read-aloud conducted by the librarian or classroom teacher. After students have conducted their quick draws for each page, reread the text and show them each illustration in the book. Ask students to discuss their own illustrations, noting similarities and differences to the book. Encourage students to talk about the feelings that are portrayed in their self-created illustrations.

Post-Reading Activities

Writing Your Feelings

Information Literacy Standards for Student Learning: 1, 3, 5, 9

NCTE/IRA Standards for the English Language Arts: 1, 3, 4, 9, 10, 11, 12

Each day give students five to ten minutes to respond to writing prompts. This will give students a chance to express themselves through writing. Have students use a small spiral notebook or a bound writing book. Instruct students to choose one of the sentence starters below to begin their journal entry for the day or select a topic and write it on the board. Students who want to share their writing should be given a chance to do so.

- My happiest day was when . . .
- I remember a time when we . . .
- I think of you whenever I . . .
- Grandma would always say . . .
- If I had a chance to tell you something, . . .
- The last time I talked about this, we . . .
- I think of you when . . .
- You always made me laugh when . . .
- I cry when . . .
- I am sad when . . .
- I am happy when . . .

Drawing Your Feelings

Information Literacy Standards for Student Learning: 1, 3, 5, 9

NCTE/IRA Standards for the English Language Arts: 1, 3, 4, 9, 10, 11, 12

Allow students to share Everett's feelings or feelings they've experienced when faced with a tragic event in their own lives. Make a class list on the board or chart paper. This list can be used as reference during the activity. Give each pair or small group of students butcher paper the length of their body. Each pair or group of students chooses one student to lie on the butcher paper. Using a marker, one student outlines the lying student's body. Each pair or group of students will have an outline of a human body on their paper. Next, each pair or group of students draw, without any words or letters, what it feels like to lose someone they love. For instance, students may say that it feels like having a broken heart. Students would represent this feeling by drawing a heart with a break down the middle. Students are not permitted to use any words in their creations, only pictures or symbols. This will encourage students to talk about the feelings involved in addition to choosing their words wisely. Once groups have created their drawings, ask students to share their illustrations with the class. This will provide an opportunity for students to relate to each other and develop empathy for others. Encourage students to make personal connections when appropriate.

Writing for Impact/Haiku Writing

Information Literacy Standards for Student Learning: 1, 3, 4, 5, 9

NCTE/IRA Standards for the English Language Arts: 1, 3, 4, 5, 6, 9, 10, 11, 12

Lucille Clifton uses few words to portray the message of hope and healing in this text. Challenge students to do the same. In pairs or small groups ask students to brainstorm how they could use few words to help someone heal after losing someone special. Some students may have personal experiences that lend to this activity. Use the following questions to help guide students:

1. What words can you use to help someone begin to heal after losing someone special?

2. What actions can someone take to begin the healing process?

3. How would you help a person who is grieving?

From this discussion, ask students to write a Haiku. A Haiku is a poem, which usually doesn't rhyme, from Japanese culture and has specific guidelines. The first line contains five (5) syllables, the second line contains seven (7) syllables, and the third line contains five (5) syllables. A Haiku should "paint" a mental image in the reader's mind by using finely chosen adjectives to create imagery. Each line must relate to each other. Have students type the poems on the computer. Additionally, students can illustrate their Haiku. Use the Haiku Rubric found in Figure 3.1 as an assessment tool. Distribute the rubric to students before they begin to write their first drafts.

Figure 3.1: Haiku Rubric

Haiku Rubric

Writer's Name(s):_____

Category	4	3	2	1
Haiku Poetry Form	The poem has 3 lines, with the proper number of syllables in each line: 5 , 7, 5	The poem has 3 lines, 2 of which have the correct syllable count.	The poem has 3 lines, but only 1 line has the correct number of syllables.	The poem has 3 lines, but no lines have the correct syllable count.
Structure: Line Relationship	Lines relate to each other in an obvious manner.	Second line does not relate to first; third line relates to second.	Second line does not relate to first, and third line does not relate to second.	Lines do not appear to be about the same subject; content does not relate to each other at all.
Language: Imagery	Vivid and superb imagery.	Effective imagery.	Vague or unfocused imagery.	Imagery not apparent.
Subject	Poem presents an everyday, personal experience with nature.	Poem presents an everyday, possible experience with nature.	Poem presents an event in nature not personal, not every day.	Poem presents an experience that is not about nature.
Mechanics	No errors in spelling, capitalization, punctuation and/or grammar.	1 error in spelling, capitalization, punctuation and/or grammar.	2 errors in spelling, capitalization, punctuation and/or grammar.	3 errors in spelling, capitalization, punctuation and/or grammar.

Becoming a Children's Book Author

Information Literacy Standards for Student Learning: 1, 2, 3, 4, 5, 9

NCTE/IRA Standards for the English Language Arts: 1, 2, 3, 4, 5, 6, 7, 8, 9, 10, 11, 12

Using the information gathered from the *Writing for Impact* activity above, challenge students to create children's books similar to Lucille Clifton's books. With few words and illustrations authors have the ability to teach and touch their readers in amazing ways. Students can work in groups to do the same. Ask students to create a picture book for children on a topic of their choice, but the topic should help children to solve a problem or overcome an obstacle. For instance, students can write a book for children who are struggling with divorce or the loss of a pet. For students who do not consider themselves artists, encourage them to create illustrations with the computer or by using magazine photographs. Share a variety of children's books with students so they can evaluate format and page layout. This will help them with their own creation. Once books have been completed on the computer, laminate the pages and bind with string. As a class, visit an elementary school or library and share the books with children. At the end of the sharing sessions, donate the books to the children's collection. The Neighborhood Picture Book Rubric in Figure 2.2 (found in Chapter 2) can be used for assessment of this assignment as well. As an alternative, students can create flipbooks via <www.readwritethink.org/materials/flipbook> or students can record their creations at <www.gcast.com> for younger students to download and listen.

Additional Information about the Author

Lucille Clifton is an author, poet, storyteller, college professor, mother of six, and a grandmother. Seven of her picture books with Henry Holt feature Everett Anderson, including *Everett Anderson's Goodbye* (a Coretta Scott King Award winner), *Everett Anderson's Nine Months Long*, *One of the Problems of Everett Anderson*, and *Everett Anderson's Christmas Coming*. In 1969 Clifton's first book, a collection of poetry titled *Good Times*, was published; in that year it was listed by *The New York Times* as one of the year's "Ten Best Books." While a college professor she wrote *Good News about the Earth* (1972) and *An Ordinary Woman* (1974). Clifton's later poetry collections include *Next: New Poems* (1987), *Quilting: Poems 1987-1990* (1991), and *The Terrible Stories* (1996). *Generations: A Memoir* (1976) is a piece celebrating her origins, and *Good Woman: Poems and a Memoir: 1969-1980* (1987) is a collection of some of her previously published work.

Electronic Resources

The Dr. Spock Company. 2005.
Retrieved on October 20, 2008 from <www.drspock.com>.

Dr. Spock offers developmentally appropriate information about talking to children about death to help them cope with the loss so that they can continue being happy, healthy children.

Tousley, M. (2000). 2000. *Grief healing*. Retrieved on October 20, 2008 from <http://griefhealing.com>.

Provides an extensive list of links in categories such as death of an infant, child, grandchild, parent, and sibling. Also provides general bereavement resources and information.

Books

Dougy Center for Grieving Children. (1999). *35 Ways to Help a Grieving Child*. Dougy Center.

This guidebook provides practical suggestions on how to support grieving children. It discusses what behaviors and reactions to expect from children at different ages and ways to create safe outlets for children to express their feelings.

Johnson, J. (1999). *Keys to Helping Children Deal with Death and Grief*. Barron's Educational Series.

This easy-to-read book guides parents, teachers, and other caregivers through the fundamental aspects of dealing with grieving children. The book tackles such subjects as explaining death, the funeral, and religion and grief simply and compassionately. This book received a 2000 Parents' Choice Award.

Kolenick, P., & Bernadowski, C. (2007). *Teaching with Books That Heal: Authentic Literature and Literacy Strategies to Help Children Cope with Everyday Problems*. Ohio: Linworth Publishing.

This handbook for classroom teachers and librarians offers book titles and ready-to-use lesson plans with reproducibles for popular children's books that deal with topics such as death of a family member, divorce, bullying, and much more.

CHAPTER 4

The People Could Fly: American Black Folktales

Bibliographic Information

Title: *The People Could Fly: American Black Folktales*

Author(s): Virginia Hamilton

Copyright: 1985

Publisher: Alfred A. Knopf

1986 Coretta Scott King Award Winner

Annotation

Many of the African-American stories in this collection were told among slaves as they remembered their lives in Africa or dreamt of being free. Several themes are presented in this text including animal tales, magical and supernatural tales, and tales of freedom. An explanation of the story selection is provided at the end of each tale. These folktales can successfully be used alone or as a complete collection.

Grade Level: Young Adult   **ISBN:** 0679843361

Discussion Starters/Writing Prompts/Pre-Reading Activities

Four folktales are included in this anthology. Before reading any of the selections, the following activities are suggested.

Spirituals

Information Literacy Standards for Student Learning: 1, 2, 3, 4, 5, 6, 7, 8, 9

NCTE/IRA Standards for the English Language Arts: 1, 2, 3, 4, 5, 6, 7, 8, 9, 10, 11, 12

Have students visit <http://www.negrospirituals.com/>to learn about the history of Negro spirituals. Additionally, students can listen to Negro spirituals on the Web site. This will give students the necessary background knowledge to comprehend American Black folktales. Require students to answer the questions below by writing the answers in their journals.

1. What purpose did spirituals serve for slaves? Describe the risks that slaves took to partake in church services.

2. Describe a Negro spiritual song. What importance do the words have in a historical context?

3. Describe the Black Renaissance. What impact did it have on Negro spirituals?

4. Describe the creation of Gospel music.

5. Why do you think music was such a large part of the African-American culture during slavery and after slavery was abolished? Describe how music affects your life.

Informal assessment of writing can be accomplished by engaging students in a classroom discussion.

Timeline

Information Literacy Standards for Student Learning: 1, 2, 3, 4, 5, 6, 7, 8, 9

NCTE/IRA Standards for the English Language Arts: 1, 2, 3, 4, 5, 6, 7, 8, 9, 10, 11, 12

Put students in small groups and require them to create a timeline of African-American History. Make this timeline large enough to hang on a wall or bulletin board so that students can use it as a reference while reading the folktales. A good place to begin research for an African-American History timeline is at PBS.org <www.pbs.org/wnet/aaworld/timeline. html>. Assign each small group of students a particular time period to research using multiple sources. Before hanging the timeline on the wall or bulletin board, ask students to share their findings with the entire class. Once all students have presented their findings, piece the timeline together for display on the classroom or library wall or bulletin board. Multiple sources may include Web sites, books, personal journals, and audio and video recordings. Use the Timeline Group Participation Checklist in Figure 4.1 to assess students' contributions to the group project. Students can use this as a self-assessment as well. Students can also view additional information at The Library of Congress at <http://memory.loc.gov/ammem/collections/voices>

Timeline Group Participation Checklist

Directions: Place a check next to "yes" or "no" for each question provided.

Used multiple sources   _____ yes   _____ no

Worked on assigned task(s) regularly   _____ yes   _____ no

Prepared for each meeting/class   _____ yes   _____ no

Met with group regularly   _____ yes   _____ no

Accurate historical information   _____ yes   _____ no

Worked well with members of the group   _____ yes   _____ no

Assignment on time   _____ yes   _____ no

Respected oneself and group members   _____ yes   _____ no

Literacy Strategies for During Reading

Discussion Questions/Journal Writing

Information Literacy Standards for Student Learning: 1, 2, 3, 4, 9

NCTE/IRA Standards for the English Language Arts: 1, 2, 4, 6, 9, 10, 11, 12

Be sure students read the introduction of the text, which provides valuable information that will aid in comprehension of the stories. Use the list below for discussion questions or journal writing prompts.

1. Describe the use of dialect that Virginia Hamilton uses. Why might she choose to use her words in the way that she does?

2. Discuss the importance of oral storytelling. What stories have been handed down from generation to generation in your own family? Share one of those stories.

3. Discuss the characteristics of folktales. Do the stories in this text follow the same format as other folktales you have read or heard?

4. How do the illustrations add to your understanding of the text? What, if any, other illustrations could have been used?

5. Pick one story and relate it to a story of a slave. What character(s) represents the master? What character(s) represent the slaves? Who is the hero in the story and why do you think this is so?

6. Pick one story and describe, in your own words, the moral of the story. Can you relate it to your own experiences in some way? Explain how this might be true.

Post-Reading Activities

The Award Goes To . . .

Information Literacy Standards for Student Learning: 1, 2, 3, 4, 5, 6, 7, 8, 9

NCTE/IRA Standards for the English Language Arts: 1, 2, 3, 4, 5, 6, 9, 10, 11, 12

The People Could Fly: American Black Folktales was given many awards including ALA Notable Children's Book, Booklist Editor's Choice, Coretta Scott King Award, The Horn Book Fanfare Honor Book, NCTE Teacher's Choice, New York Times Best Illustrated Book, Notable Children's Trade Book in the Field of Social Studies, Parent's Choice Award Recording, Read-Aloud Handbook Selection, and School Library Journal Best Book of the Year. Ask small groups of students to pick one of the awards and research its history and criteria for selection. The librarian or classroom teacher may want to assign awards to specific groups. Students research the award and provide a historical background as well as criteria for selection. Students then design a seal for that award. It cannot resemble the current award seal, if applicable. Finally, students find another quality book and award their seal to the new selection. This book must meet the criteria for the award. Have students present the information to the class. Display the newly awarded book with the "new seal" attached. Display the books in the library book case or other high traffic area. This may encourage someone to read that book for the first time. This activity is designed to encourage students to read additional books. The Award Seal Rubric found in Figure 4.2 can be used for assessment purposes.

Figure 4.2: Award Seal Rubric

Name(s):_____

Award Seal Rubric

Category	2	1	0
Criteria Selection	Extensive criteria selection was used.	Adequate criteria selection was used.	Less than adequate criteria selection was used.
Mechanics	There are 0-2 errors in capitalization, punctuation, and/or grammar.	There are 3-5 errors in capitalization, punctuation, and/or grammar.	There are 6 or more errors in capitalization, punctuation, and/or grammar.
Historical Background	An extensive historical background on the original seal was apparent.	Background on the original seal was apparent.	Lacked background on original seal.
Original Design	The design was original and highly creative. It is apparent that the group worked collaboratively to make a presentable product.	The design was somewhat original. The design was a presentable product.	The design was not original and elements from other seals were apparent. It was not ready for presentation.
Presentation to Classmates	All group members contributed to the presentation of the seal to classmates. The presentation was clear, highly organized and presented in a professional manner.	All group members contributed to the presentation of the seal to classmates. The presentation was somewhat clear and organized. The presentation was not as polished as it could have been.	Not all group members contributed to the presentation of the seal to classmates. The presentation is either unorganized or unclear in its purpose. Needs improvement to be ready for presentation to an audience.

Writing a Folktale

Information Literacy Standards for Student Learning: 1, 2, 3, 4, 5, 6, 7, 8, 9

NCTE/IRA Standards for the English Language Arts: 1, 2, 3, 4, 5, 6, 9, 10, 11, 12

Require students to write a modern day folktale using common proverbs from African culture. The following is a list of proverbs from which students can choose or allow students to find a proverb of their own.

* A wise man never knows all, only fools know everything.

* Indecision is like a stepchild: if he does not wash his hands, he is called dirty, if he does, he is wasting water.

* Only a fool tests the depth of the water with both feet.

* Whatever accomplishments you boast of in the world, there is someone better than you.

* Do not look where you fell, but where you slipped.

Once students have chosen a proverb to use as the basis for their folktale, require students to brainstorm before writing using the Story Map in Figure 4.3. Students complete the story map prior to writing a rough draft. After the rough draft is complete, students meet with a peer for editing and revising purposes. Finally, students create a final draft using a word processing program. Bind each story into a class book using string. This compilation can be distributed to each member of the class and shelved in the library. The Folktale Rubric in Figure 4.4 can be used to assess students' written work.

Figure 4.3: Story Map

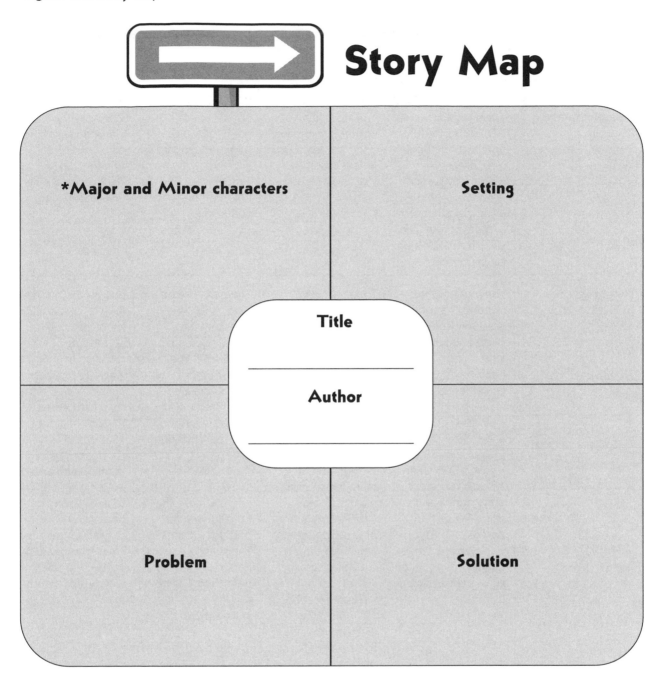

Story Map

*Major and Minor characters

Setting

Title

_____

Author

_____

Problem

Solution

Plot Development

_____

_____

_____

*Not all stories will have minor characters

Figure 4.4: Folktale Rubric

Writer's Name(s):_____

	4	3	2	1
Organization	The story has a clear beginning, middle, and end. The beginning engages readers by presenting them with details of characters, setting, or plot. The story follows a logical sequence.	The story has a beginning, middle, and end, and events follow in some logical sequence.	The story does not have a clear beginning, middle, and end. The sequence of events is sometimes confusing.	The story is missing either a beginning or an end. The relationship between events is often confusing.
Elements of Fiction	The plot is interesting, and the conflict is established, developed, and resolved after a gripping climax. Most characters are well-developed through dialogue, actions, and thoughts. Dialogue sounds realistic. Main characters change or grow during the story. The setting is described through vivid sensory language. The point of view is consistent.	The plot makes sense, and the conflict is established, developed and resolved after a climax. Some characters are well-developed through dialogue, actions, and thoughts. Most dialogue sounds realistic. Main characters change or grow during the story. The setting is clear and some sensory language is used to describe it. The point of view is clear, but may be inconsistent in places.	The plot may be hard to follow. The conflict is established and resolved, but it lacks development. The characters are described rather than established through dialogue, action, and thoughts. They show little growth or change. Dialogue for all characters may sound similar. The setting is identified but not clearly described. The point of view is often inconsistent.	The plot is hard to follow. The conflict is not developed and it may not be resolved in a logical way. The characters are described rather than established through dialogue, action, and thoughts. They lack individuality and do not change. Dialogue may be nonexistent, or it may all sound alike. The setting may be vague. The point of view keeps shifting.
Grammar, Usage, Mechanics, and Spelling	There are few or no errors in mechanics, usage, grammar, or spelling. Dialogue is punctuated and formatted correctly.	There are some errors in mechanics, usage, grammar, or spelling. Dialogue may have minor errors in punctuation or format.	There are many errors in mechanics, usage, grammar, or spelling. These sometimes make the story hard to understand. Dialogue is punctuated and formatted inconsistently.	Numerous errors in mechanics, usage, grammar, and spelling interfere with meaning. Dialogue may be indistinguishable from narrative, or it may lack essential element, such as quotation marks or end punctuation.

Exploring Slave Narratives through Diary Writing

Information Literacy Standards for Student Learning: 1, 2, 3, 4, 5, 6, 7, 8, 9

NCTE/IRA Standards for the English Language Arts: 1, 2, 3, 4, 5, 6, 9, 10, 11, 12

Require students to use the Web site <www.umsl.edu/~libweb/blackstudies/moslave.htm> to read numerous slave narratives. Once students have explored the slave narratives, have them write a diary entry for five consecutive days as if they were a slave themselves. Allow students to explore additional resources that may be helpful. Students should include an accurate date at the top of each page. Remind students they are writing from a slave's point of view. Use the Slave Narrative Rubric in Figure 4.5 for assignment guidelines and assessment purposes. Allow students to use dialect that would ring true of slave language during that time period.

Figure 4.5: Slave Narrative Rubric

Name(s):_____

Slave Narrative Rubric

Category	2	1	0
Historical Accuracy	All entries are historically accurate based on the date of each entry.		Not all entries are historically accurate based on the date of each entry.
Point of View	All entries are told from the first person point of view.	Some entries are told from the first person point of view.	All entries are not told from the first person point of view.
Date	Each entry includes an accurate date at the top of the entry.	Some entries include an accurate date at the top of the entry.	No entries include an accurate date at the top of the entry.
Five Consecutive Days	Five entries are included in consecutive order.	Five entries are included but are not in consecutive order.	Does not include five entries.

Readers Theatre

Information Literacy Standards for Student Learning: 1, 2, 3, 4, 5, 6, 7, 8, 9

NCTE/IRA Standards for the English Language Arts: 1, 2, 3, 4, 5, 6, 9, 10, 11, 12

Readers theatre is a literacy strategy that helps students improve their writing and reading skills. By practicing their part of the script over a period of time, students increase their oral reading fluency performance. Furthermore, students who write their own scripts have the advantage of honing their writing skills for an audience. Moreover, students improve their comprehension of the text and have fun while learning.

Assign one story in the collection to a small group of students. The book has four sections. Section one is "Animal Tales," which includes seven stories; section two is "Real, Extravagant, and Fanciful," which includes six stories; section three is "Supernatural," which includes five stories; and section four is "Slaves Tales of Freedom," which includes six stories. An alternative is to allow each group of students to choose one story from one of the sections. Instruct students that they will write a script and perform the script for the class or for elementary students or other audiences. Typically, this project could take one to two weeks to develop and execute. Students first choose the story and begin to write the script. Students must identify the speaking parts or main characters of the story. Once this is accomplished, they begin to use the dialogue from the text as the speaking parts for each character. For example, on page 6 of *He Lion, Bruh Bear, and Bruh Rabbit*, the text states "Why he Lion want to do that?" Bruh Bear said. "Is that all he Lion have to say?" Bruh Rabbit asked. "We don't know why, but that's all the Lion can tell us and we didn't ask him to tell us that," said the little animals. Model for students the format of a script by showing them how to use those lines in script form.

Bruh Bear: Why he Lion want to do that?

Bruh Rabbit: Is that all he Lion have to say?

Squirrel and Possum: We don't know why, but that's all the Lion can tell us and we didn't ask him to tell us that.

It is important to note that students may have to reread the text several times in order to prepare their scripts adequately, which improves reading fluency and comprehension. Once scripts are written, require each group to assign reading parts and practice reading the material. It is important to tell students that it is not necessary to memorize parts, but to concentrate on reading with emphasis, appropriate intonation, and audience engagement. Requiring students to "perform" or read to an audience may give students the extra encouragement to sharpen their reading performance.

Additional Information about the Author

Virginia Hamilton has published countless books for children and teens, and is sometimes referred to as "America's most honored writer of books for children." Her most recent publications include *The Girl Who Spun Gold*; *Bluish: A Novel*; and *Second Cousins*. Hamilton died in 2002.

Electronic Resources

Virginia Hamilton (2001). Hamilton Arts, Inc. 27 August 2008 <http://www.virginia-hamilton.com/>.

The official Web site of Virginia Hamilton offers readers and fans countless resources and access to insider information about the beloved author.

Virginia Hamilton. Highlights Teachers' Net. 17 August 2008 <http://falcon.jmu.edu/~ramseyil/hamilton.htm>.

Read a brief biography or explore the many links about author Virginia Hamilton.

American Slave Narratives: An Online Anthology. 6 March 1988. University of Virginia. 13 August 2008 <http://xroads.virginia.edu/~hyper/wpa/wpahome.html>.

An annotated index of slave narratives can be accessed from this site maintained by the University of Virginia. Related resources are also readily available for students. Additionally, a note about how to read the narratives is provided that students should read prior to reading the narratives.

Born into Slavery: Slave Narratives from the Federal Writers' Project, 1936-1938. 23 March 2001. Library of Congress. 13 August 2008 <http://memory.loc.gov/ammem/collections/voices>.

This comprehensive resource of slave narratives sustained by the Library of Congress contains slave narrative manuscripts and slave photographs. A keyword search is accessible on this all-inclusive site.

Books

Gates, H. L. (2002). *The Classic Slave Narratives*. New York: Signet Classic.

Along with the writings of Frederick Douglas and Olaudah Equiano, this anthology includes the writings of women slaves Harriet Jacobs and Mary Prince.

Hamilton, V. (1999). *Bluish: A Novel*. New York: Blue Sky Press.

A young adult story about a girl who looks different than her classmates and struggles to fit into a group.

Hamilton, V. (2000). *The Girl Who Spun Gold*. New York: Scholastic.

In this West Indian version of the Rumpelstiltskin story, Lit'mahn spins thread into gold cloth for the king's new bride.

Hamilton, V. (1984). *The House of Dies Drear*. Madison, WI: Demco Media.

A black family tries to unravel the secrets of their new home which was once a stop on the Underground Railroad.

Hamilton, V. (1997). *A Ring of Tricksters: Animal Tales from America, the West Indies and West Africa*. New York: Blue Sky Press.

Twelve trickster tales that show the migration of African culture to America via the West Indies.

Lester, J. (1994). *Black Folktales*. New York: Grove Press.

Twelve remarkable folktales about the black experience in Africa and America.

CHAPTER 5

Justin and the Best Biscuits in the World

Bibliographic Information

Title: *Justin and the Best Biscuits in the World*

Author(s): Mildred Pitts Walter

Copyright: 1986

Publisher: Harper Collins Publishers

1987 Coretta Scott King Award Winner

Annotation

Ten-year-old Justin learns important lessons when his father passes away and he is left to be the man of the house. Justin has trouble doing household chores, such as making his bed, because he thinks that is "women's work." Grandfather Ward takes Justin to his ranch where he learns that men not only do chores, but they show their emotions and sometimes even cry. Justin learns that "real cowboys" do everything from mending fences, to catching fish, to making the best biscuits in the world. This coming of age story teaches valuable life and history lessons.

Grade Level: ages 9-12   **ISBN:** 9780688066451

Discussion Starters/Writing Prompts/Pre-Reading Activities

Research Writing

Information Literacy Standards for Student Learning: 1, 2, 3, 4, 6, 7, 8, 9

NCTE/IRA Standards for the English Language Arts: 1, 3, 4, 5, 6, 7, 8, 10, 11, 12

Have students research a topic and present their findings to the class in the form of an oral report. Allow students to work in groups to research, write, and present one of the following topics:

1. Bill Picket
2. Jesse Stahl
3. History of Rodeos
4. Homestead Act
5. Calf Roping

Be sure students use multiple sources including books, articles, and the Internet. Use the Research Process Rubric in Figure 5.1 and the Oral Presentation Rubric in Figure 5.2 to assess students.

Figure 5.1: Research Project Rubric

	Beginning	Novice	Proficient	Exemplary
Defining the Topic	Student has no research question. Teacher has to supply question.	Basic research question is vague. Related questions do not help answer basic question. Student knows general subject matter to be searched.	Basic research question is focused and clear. Most related questions focus topic.	Basic research question is clear, complete, and requires critical thinking skills. Related questions focus topic accurately.
Collecting Information	Information is not accurate or complete. Student does not meet the required number or sources.	Student uses the minimal number of sources. Information frequently does not relate to questions.	Student efficiently determines the appropriate sources for information and uses multiple, varied sources. Most information relates directly to the questions.	Student utilizes a variety of resources and only the information that answers the research question is used. Search strategies are revised as information is located or could not be found.
Evaluating Sources	Only one type of source is used.	Two or more types of sources are used.	Multiple types of sources are used and reflect support of the essential and related questions.	Diverse sources are used and reflect support of the essential questions. Student compares information from at least two sources.
Extracting Information	Contains missing details and isn't completely accurate. Questions are unanswered.	Incomplete, only one related question is answered. Student can summarize information source but missed some concepts.	Answers the questions in a way that reflects learning using some detail and accuracy.	Student assesses information in a meaningful way and creates a product that clearly answers the questions with accuracy, detail, and understanding. Student determines if information supports or rejects student's thesis.
Citing Information	Sources are not cited properly.	MLA format is followed although several errors are apparent.	MLA format is followed. Student lists most of the components in correct form.	MLA format is exact. No errors are evident.
Reflecting on Research	Student is disorganized, does not have a research strategy, and does not use time effectively.	Student needs considerable teacher help to organize research. Some steps are missing in the plan.	Student works within the time frame and develops a system to organize information. Requires some teacher help.	Time management skills are excellent. Student develops a clear method to organize information and makes revisions in plan when needed.

North High School Library/Community Library, District 99 in Downers Grove, IL. Reprinted with permission.

Oral Presentation Rubric

Performance Indicator	3	2	1	0
Eye Contact	Constantly looks at someone or some groups at all time; rarely uses notes.	Occasionally looks at someone or some groups at all times; occasionally uses notes.	Only focuses attention to one particular part of the class or audience; relies on notes.	Does not attempt to make eye contact with audience; reads notes the entire time.
Facial Expressions and Gestures	Appropriate expression is used and natural gestures are demonstrated throughout the speech.			Displays no expressions and no gestures during presentations.
Posture	Stands up straight during the entire presentation.	Occasionally slumps during the presentation.	Slumps throughout most of the presentation.	Sits or slumps during the entire presentation.
Introduction	Includes a comprehensive and logical introduction; the audience clearly understands the topic of the report.	Includes a logical introduction; the audience understands the topic of the report.	Vaguely informs audience of the topic of the report and/or does not include a logical introduction.	Does not inform the audience of the topic of the report and does not include a logical introduction.
Content	Comprehensive explanation of content covering all points.	Explanation of content is good and the presenter covers all points.	Majority of points glossed over and not covered thoroughly.	Much content is left out of the presentation and glossed over.
Professionalism	Presentation is superior. It is well organized, thorough, and keeps the attention of the audience.	Presentation is good. It is organized, thorough, and keeps the attention of the audience.	Presentation is somewhat disorganized and/or does not keep the attention of the audience.	Presentation is disorganized and does not keep the attention of the audience.

Total: _____

Family Tree

Information Literacy Standards for Student Learning: 1, 2, 3, 4, 6, 7, 8, 9

NCTE/IRA Standards for the English Language Arts: 1, 3, 4, 5, 6, 7, 8, 10, 11, 12

Justin learns about the history of his family while spending time with his grandpa on his ranch. Much of what Justin learned from his grandpa was through stories, both written and oral. Require students to research their own genealogy and create a family tree. Have students create their family tree using the Family Tree Template in Figure 5.3. As an alternative, allow students to create their family tree using a program such an Inspiration©, Kidspiration©, or a word processing program. Once students have created their family tree, require them to write a descriptive paragraph about each family member on the tree. Information about family members may have to be obtained through interviews and family photographs.

Figure 5.3: Family Tree Template

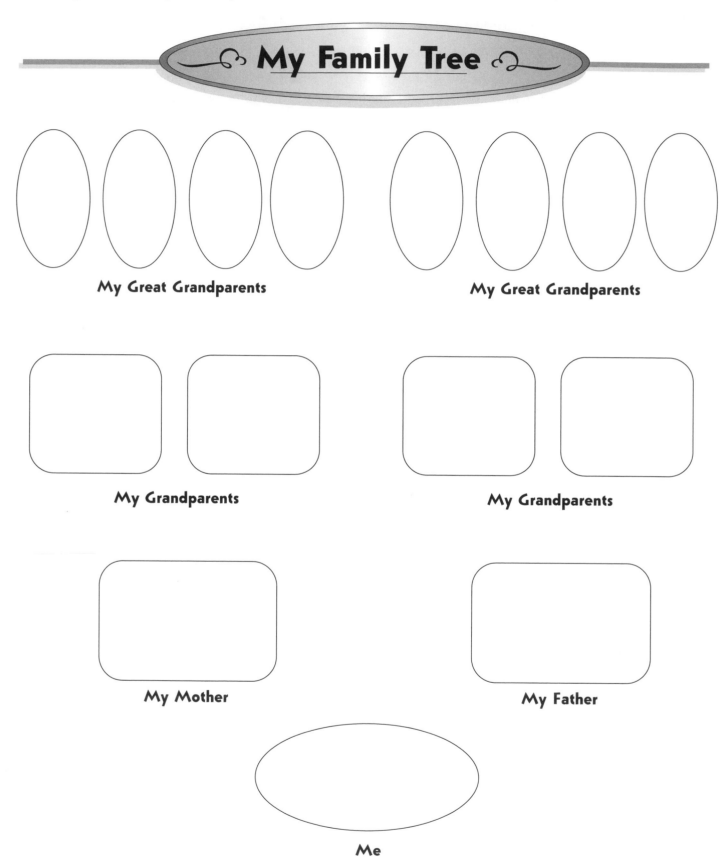

Teaching Literacy Skills to Adolescents Using Coretta Scott King Award Winners

Literacy Strategies for During Reading

Questions to Guide Reading

Information Literacy Standards for Student Learning: 1, 2, 3, 4, 9

NCTE/IRA Standards for the English Language Arts: 1, 2, 4, 6, 9, 10, 11, 12

1. Describe the characters you meet in chapter one. Make a list of qualities for each.

2. Justin secretly wished he had a brother in the beginning of the book. Why do you think this is so? Have you ever wished you had a brother or sister?

3. Describe what happens to Justin's father. How does he react? How would you react?

4. Write a paragraph that describes Grandpa.

Similes

Information Literacy Standards for Student Learning: 1, 2, 3, 6

NCTE/IRA Standards for the English Language Arts: 1, 3, 4, 5, 6, 11, 12

On page 17 the reader encounters the simile "neat as a pin." Require students to find three additional similes from the text. Next, have students illustrate or create on the computer their similes and share with the class. Students should be certain as to the meanings of their similes. If they cannot find three additional similes in the text, allow them to create their own. By listening to students read their similes, the librarian or classroom teacher can informally assess comprehension and mastery of skill.

Post-Reading Activities

Scrapbooking

Information Literacy Standards for Student Learning: 1, 2, 3

NCTE/IRA Standards for the English Language Arts: 1, 3, 4, 5, 6, 8, 9, 11, 12

Have students create a scrapbook page for Justin's father before he was in a car accident. Include pictures from magazines, the Internet or allow students to draw pictures. Ask students to include captions of their photos and explain their page to the class. This exercise will allow students to demonstrate their interpretation and understanding of the main character.

Literal vs. Inferential Meanings

Information Literacy Standards for Student Learning: 1, 2

NCTE/IRA Standards for the English Language Arts: 1, 3, 4, 5, 6, 11, 12

Justin learns about mending fences, both the literal and inferential meaning, in the book. Challenge students to find other words or phrases that have both literal and inferential meanings. Have students use the Literal vs. Inferential Meaning reproducible found in Figure 5.4 to collect words or phrases that have double meanings and share them with the class. A collection can be written on butcher paper and displayed in the library or classroom. Allowing students to discuss the various words and their meanings will provide the librarian or classroom teacher significant evidence of understanding. Any misconceptions or misinterpretations can be discussed with the class.

Literal vs. Inferential Meaning

Word or Phrase	Literal Meaning	Inferential Meaning

Comparison Using a Venn diagram

Information Literacy Standards for Student Learning: 1, 2, 3

NCTE/IRA Standards for the English Language Arts: 1, 3, 4, 5, 6, 11, 12

After students read the book, ask them to use the Venn diagram provided in Figure 5.5 to compare themselves to Justin. Lead a discussion about how many readers relate to the characters that they read about in books. The ability to relate to the characters gives readers a deeper understanding of the text overall. Additionally, the librarian or teacher can make a class Venn diagram on butcher paper and allow students to write their similarities and differences directly on the class Venn diagram. As an alternative, students can create a Venn diagram using a word processing program on the computer.

Figure 5.4: Venn diagram

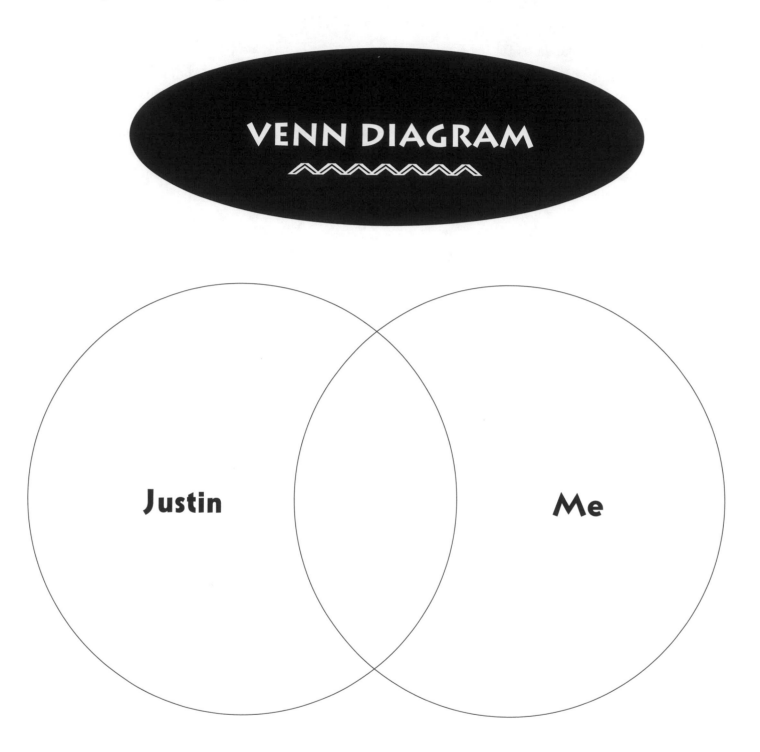

Women's Work/Men's Work

Information Literacy Standards for Student Learning: 1, 2, 3

NCTE/IRA Standards for the English Language Arts: 1, 3, 4, 5, 6, 11, 12

Justin doesn't want to clean his bedroom because he thinks it is women's work and should not be completed by a male. Prompt students to make a class list of other jobs or duties that students believe are characteristic of a job performed by either a woman or a man. Discuss stereotypes with students and challenge them to devise solutions to these misconceptions. For example, changing a tire on a car may be stereotypical of work performed by a man. Play devil's advocate and provide reasons why women are just as capable as men to change a car's tire. A further discussion of equal opportunity may pursue from this initial discussion.

Creating a Festival Poster

Information Literacy Standards for Student Learning: 1, 2, 3, 6

NCTE/IRA Standards for the English Language Arts: 1, 3, 4, 5, 6, 7, 8, 11, 12

Justin enjoys attending the festival with Grandpa. Ask students to create a poster for the festival based on the descriptions found in the book.

Creating a Dust Cover

Information Literacy Standards for Student Learning: 1, 2, 3, 6

NCTE/IRA Standards for the English Language Arts: 1, 3, 4, 5, 6, 7, 8, 11, 12

Review the cover of the book, noting the relationship between the title and the accompanying illustration. Require students to create a new dust cover. The front cover should include the title, author, illustrator (if applicable), and new illustration. Next, have students write a summary of the book for the inside cover. Furthermore, students can write reviews for the inside back cover. The back of the book can display additional book titles written by the author, as well as a brief biography. Finally, have students present the new cover to the class. Use the Dust Cover Checklist in Figure 5.6 for assessment purposes.

Name(s):_____

Dust Cover Checklist

Criteria	Yes (5 points)	No (0 points)
Student(s) includes all indentifying information such as title, author, illustrator (if applicable), and new illustration.		
Summary included on the inside cover. The summary is accurate and free from errors in spelling, punctuation and mechanics.		
Reviews are included in the back cover. Student(s) make an effort to include several summaries with vivid language to entice readers.		
Additional book titles by the author are included.		

Total: _____

Additional Information about the Author

Mildred Pitts has been a teacher, wife, women's and civil rights activist, book reviewer, and children's book author. She has won the Coretta Scott King Award three times. Other book titles include *The Girl on the Outside* and *Have a Happy,* a book about a boy whose December 25 birthday often gets forgotten in the holiday rush. She now makes her home in Denver, Colorado.

Additional Resources

Electronic Resources

McRae, B. J. (2008) Black cowboys also worked on the ranches and rode the cattle trails. Retrieved on September 4, 2008 from <www.coax.net/people/1wf/bkcwboys.htm>.

This article provides an in-depth investigation on the life of black cowboys.

Shepherd, B. (2008) History of Buffalo Soldiers. Retrieved on September 9, 2008 from <www.geocities.com/cott1388/black-cowboy.html>.

This site includes countless links to articles, Web pages, books and much more.

Slatta, R. (2008). African-American Cowboys. Retrieved on September 5, 2008 from <http://social.chass.ncsu.edu/slatta/essays/blackcowboys.htm>.

Information about African-American Cowboys, including Bill Pickett, can be found on this Web site.

Books

Katz, W. L. (1995). *Black Women of the Old West.* New York: Atheneum.

This book portrays the role that black women had during America's westward expansion.

Katz, W. L. (2005). *The Black West: A Documentary and Pictorial History of the African-American Role in the Westward Expansion of the United States.* New York: Harlem Moon.

Fabulous photographs and text highlight the important role that African Americans played in our early frontiers.

CHAPTER 6

Bibliographic Information

Title: *Fallen Angels*

Author(s): Walter Dean Myers

Copyright: 1987

Publisher: Scholastic Paperbacks

1989 Coretta Scott King Award Winner

Annotation

When Parry's dream of attending college isn't fulfilled, he enlists in the U.S. Army during the Vietnam War. The front lines of war are portrayed and readers begin to understand the horrific truth of warfare. Perry struggles to be a soldier, a friend, a brother, and a son while dealing with the realities of war. Myers accurately portrays a war that changed a nation of young men. The action is extremely fast-paced and realistic, and his characters are quite memorable as he weaves war and personal conflict into one. Myers dedicates this book to his brother who died in Vietnam on May 7, 1968.

Grade Level: ages 13 and up (young adult)   **ISBN:** 978-0590409438

Discussion Starters/Writing Prompts/Pre-Reading Activities
KWL/Vietnam Research

Information Literacy Standards for Student Learning: 1, 2, 3, 4, 6, 7, 8, 9

NCTE/IRA Standards for the English Language Arts: 1, 3, 5, 6, 11, 12

Students may come to this text knowing much or little about the Vietnam War. It is essential to discuss what students know about the topic prior to reading. Use the **KWL Chart** in Figure 6.1 as a way to prompt students' background knowledge and prior experience. Have students complete the **K** (What I **Know**) column individually. Then, ask students to share their background knowledge with the class. After class discussion, document on the chalkboard all student responses. Then allow students to complete the **W** (What I **Want** to Learn) column. Students will use the W column as a starting point for their individual research on the Vietnam War. Require students to use three sources, two electronic and one print, to find information related to the Vietnam War to present to the class. Make a class list of facts so that students can refer to it during the reading. Students may discover that many of their facts from column one were really misconceptions or in need of refinement or confirmation. The Vietnam War was a controversial war, and some students may have invalid or incomplete information. The research process will allow students to discover these misconceptions or incomplete facts. Finally, have students complete the **L** (What I **Learned**) column after their research has been completed. The last column requires students to document their learning.

Figure 6.1: KWL Chart

KWL: VIETNAM WAR

K (What I Know)	W (What I Want to Learn)	L (What I Learned)

Vocabulary Notebook

Information Literacy Standards for Student Learning: 1, 2, 3, 6, 9

NCTE/IRA Standards for the English Language Arts: 1, 3, 9, 11, 12

Work with students to create a Vocabulary Notebook before they read the text. The notebook will serve as a dictionary of unfamiliar terms that students encounter while reading. The notebook can be a store bought spiral notebook or paper stapled with a construction paper cover. The important part is that students keep track of terms in one central location. Have students write the word and self-created definition in the notebook that can be used as reference during reading. Instead of a dictionary as reference, require students to use context clues to define the terms when applicable. The following terms might help begin this activity: *flak jacket, shrapnel, landing zone, malaria, spider holes, claymores, ARVNs, and Viet-Cong.* Stress the importance of students finding terms that they don't know or are uncertain about the definition.

Literacy Strategies for During Reading

Character Study

Information Literacy Standards for Student Learning: 1, 2, 3, 9

NCTE/IRA Standards for the English Language Arts: 1, 3, 5, 9, 11, 12

Require students to keep a character map for prominent characters in the book. The Character Map in Figure 6.2 can be reproduced. Additions to the character maps should occur throughout the reading. Students can also work in small groups to dissect a certain character and combine their maps into one. Using a character map ensures students are paying close attention to the development of characters, which is an important element in Walter Dean Myers' writing. Characters to examine include Richard Perry, Harold Peewee Gates, Lobel, Brew, and Lieutenant Carroll.

Character Map

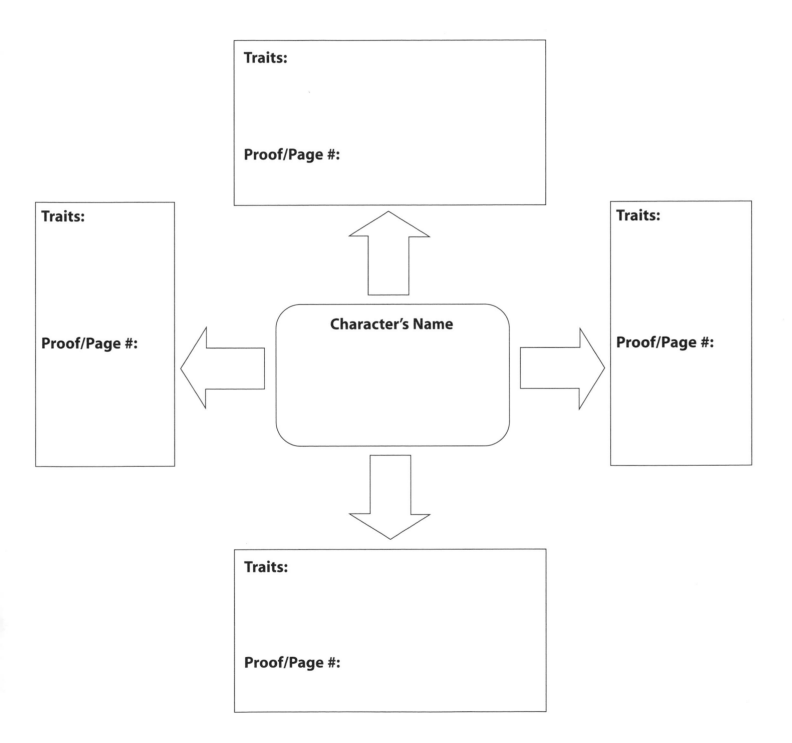

Photo Quotes

Information Literacy Standards for Student Learning: 1, 2, 3, 4, 6, 7, 8, 9

NCTE/IRA Standards for the English Language Arts: 1, 3, 4, 5, 6, 7, 8, 11, 12

Have students work in small groups of three to four and develop Photo Quotes. Students choose 10 quotes from the book that sparked their interest during their reading. Distribute the Quote Tracker in Figure 6.3. Students will use this form to keep track of the interesting quotes that they find while reading. Once students have each collected 10 quotes, groups determine the top five quotes from each member. Using the Internet, groups find a photograph, illustration, or clipart that best portrays that quote. Students then generate a PowerPoint© presentation with all quotes and photographs or illustrations. Groups will share their presentations with the class, providing background information on its relevance to the story. Require students to include a works cited section at the end of their presentation so that the audience can access photographs and illustrations of interest to them. Use the Photo Quote Rubric in Figure 6.4 for assessment purposes.

Figure 5.6: Quote Tracker

Title of Book_____

Author: _____

Page Number	Quote	Who said it?	What do you think it means?

Figure 6.4: Photo Quote Rubric

Photo Quote Rubric

Criteria	2	1	0
Quotes	Includes 10 quotes from the text.	Includes 8-9 quotes from the text.	Includes less than 8 quotes from the text.
Mechanics	There are 0-1 errors in capitalization, punctuation, and/or grammar in the electronic presentation.	There are 2-3 errors in capitalization, punctuation, and/or grammar in the electronic presentation.	There are 4 or more errors in capitalization, punctuation, and/or grammar in the electronic presentation.
APA Style	There are 0 errors in APA citation.	There are 1-2 errors in APA citation.	There are 3 or more errors in APA citation.
Summary	Students thoroughly and extensively explain the rationale and relevance of photographs/ illustrations to the story.	Students somewhat explain the rationale and relevance of photographs/ illustrations to the story.	Students do not explain the rationale and relevance of photographs/ illustrations to the story.
Presentation	Students were well-prepared for the presentation. The presentation was organized and delivery was superior.	Students were prepared for the presentation. The presentation was organized and delivery was acceptable.	Students were not prepared for the presentation. The presentation was unorganized and delivery was unacceptable.

Post-Reading Activities

Letters Home

Information Literacy Standards for Student Learning: 1, 2, 3, 4, 6, 7, 8, 9

NCTE/IRA Standards for the English Language Arts: 1, 3, 5, 6, 11, 12

Have students write a first person narrative about their experience in the Vietnam War as if they were writing a letter home to a loved one. Using multiple sources such as the Internet, books, newspaper and magazine articles, interviews, and other sources, students will synthesize the information into a first person narrative. Students must use quotes directly from their sources in their letter home. All information must be accurate. Ensure students date the letter. Finally, students must choose a hypothetical location from which they are stationed. Included with the letter home, students must supply a map of their locale. This will give the reader an understanding of the geographic location of the writer. Use the Letters Home Rubric in Figure 6.5 for assessment purposes.

Figure 6.5: Letters Home Rubric

Letters Home Rubric

Criteria	2	1	0
First Person	The letter is written from first person point of view.		The letter is not written from first person point of view.
Mechanics	There are 0-2 errors in capitalization, punctuation, and/or grammar.	There are 3-5 errors in capitalization, punctuation, and/or grammar.	There are 6 or more errors in capitalization, punctuation, and/or grammar.
Historical Accuracy	The letter is extremely historically accurate. All dates, places, and/or events are accurate and no inconsistencies exist.	The letter is somewhat historically accurate. There are one or two inconsistencies in relation to dates, places, and/or events.	The letter is historically inaccurate. There are three or more inconsistencies in relation to dates, places, and/or events.
Date and Location	Date and location are accurate.	Date OR location is accurate.	Date and location are inaccurate.
Map Included	A detailed, accurate map is included with the letter.	A map is included with the letter.	A map is not included with the letter.

War Memorial

Information Literacy Standards for Student Learning: 1, 2, 3, 6, 7, 8, 9

NCTE/IRA Standards for the English Language Arts: 1, 2, 3, 4, 5, 7, 8, 11, 12

For this activity, have students work in small groups to research various war memorials and their importance and impact on soldiers, their families, and the communities. Students will create their own war memorial for the Vietnam War that differs from any current memorials. Students can create their war memorial as a sketch, three-dimensional object, or other format that might be of interest to them.

Media Coverage

Information Literacy Standards for Student Learning: 1, 2, 3, 4, 6, 7, 8, 9

NCTE/IRA Standards for the English Language Arts: 1, 3, 5, 6, 11, 12

Have students examine the media coverage of the Vietnam War. Although technology is much more advanced today than during the Vietnam War, students should then compare the news coverage of the war in the Middle East, including both Afghanistan and Iraq. A class discussion of the similarities and differences will shed light on the multilayered facets of war and the involvement of the media.

Guest Speaker

Information Literacy Standards for Student Learning: 7, 8, 9

NCTE/IRA Standards for the English Language Arts: 4, 7, 11, 12

Invite a guest speaker to visit the classroom or library and speak about their experience in the Vietnam War. Prepare students by requiring each of them to have two questions to ask the veteran prior to the visit. After the presentation, ensure students properly thank the guest speaker with handwritten thank-you notes.

Discussion Questions/Essay Questions

Information Literacy Standards for Student Learning: 1, 2, 3, 4, 9

NCTE/IRA Standards for the English Language Arts: 1, 2, 4, 6, 9, 10, 11, 12

The following is a list of questions that can be used for class discussion, book club discussion or essay questions.

1. Discuss the transformation that takes place in Richie once he is engaged in war. How has he changed since he first enlisted in the army? Has he changed for better or for worse in your opinion? Defend your position.

2. Based on what you have learned about the Vietnam War, how does this book compare to your knowledge? Does it add to your understanding? Does it contradict what you have learned? Do you think it is accurate in its description of the war? Students can refer to the KWL chart used before reading.

3. Discuss the reasons that Richie has enlisted in the army. Are these good reasons for enlisting? Why or why not? What other reasons do young men and women enlist in the army or other armed forces?

4. Richie dreams of becoming a writer. Do you think he has what it takes? Why or why not?

5. Soldiers are faced with life or death situations daily. Discuss how you might react to the situations that the characters faced in this book.

6. Discuss how soldiers are memorialized. How should soldiers be remembered for their sacrifice for their nation?

Additional Information about the Author

Walter Dean Myers is an author of countless books for adolescent readers. He continues to write and inspire young adults to make good choices in their lives. He often speaks to groups about important issues in teens' lives. Recent titles include *Malcolm X: A Fire Burning Brightly, Monster,* and *Sunrise Over Fallujah.* Many of Myers' books have received countless awards and he is known as one of the best authors of literature for African-American teens.

Additional Resources

Electronic Resources

The Ultimate Resource for the Vietnam War. Retrieved on September 17, 2008 from <www.vietnamwar.com>.

> This Web site includes numerous historical statistics, stories, pictures, and facts about the Vietnam War. Students will find it full of valuable information for their own personal research.

Interknowledge Corporation. (2007). *An Introduction to Vietnam.* Retrieved on September 17, 2008 from <http://www.geographia.com/vietnam>.

> This Web site provides the foundation of knowledge about the Vietnam War. Hyperlinks throughout the text aid the reader with unfamiliar vocabulary.

Public Broadcasting System. (2005). *Vietnam Online—An Online Companion to Vietnam: A Television History.* Retrieved on September 17, 2008 from <http://www.pbs.org/wgbh/amex/vietnam/>.

> This excellent resource can be used as a companion to the PBS videos or individually since it provides accurate timelines, maps, primary resources, and much more. A teacher's guide is also included.

Books

Bilton, M., & Sim. K. (1993). *Four Hours in My Lai.* New York: Penguin.

> A complete account of the massacre that killed the most innocent civilians in the shortest period of time during the Vietnam conflict.

Glasser, R. (1980). *365 Days.* New York: George Braziller Inc.

> The story of an American soldier in Vietnam.

Karnow, S. (1997). *Vietnam: A History.* New York: Penguin.

> This book provides a historical summary of the Vietnam War from many perspectives including Americans, Vietnamese, French, and other nationalities.

CHAPTER 7

The Road to Memphis

Bibliographic Information

Title: *The Road to Memphis*

Author(s): Mildred D. Taylor

Copyright: 1990

Publisher: Penguin Young Readers Group

1991 Coretta Scott King Award Winner

Annotation

This text is one book in a series of books that tell the story of the Logan family. The setting of this particular book is racist Mississippi in 1941. The Road to Memphis describes three unforgettable days in the life of an African-American high school girl, Cassie Logan, who dreams of leaving Mississippi and escaping the racial tensions of her town. She will face the dark side of humanity as she faces discrimination, prejudice, and tough decisions.

Grade Level: grades 5 and up   **ISBN:** 9780140360776

Discussion Starters/Writing Prompts/Pre-Reading Activities

Family Discussion

Information Literacy Standards for Student Learning: 1, 2, 3, 4, 6, 7, 8, 9

NCTE/IRA Standards for the English Language Arts: 1, 3, 5, 6, 11, 12

Before reading the book begin a discussion of family and what the word means to students, keeping in mind that each student has their own personal experience and definition of the term. Be sure to allow students to fully express themselves in terms of their own experience with family. This is a good preface to the relationship between Cassie and Stacey that the reader encounters in the book. Ask students with siblings to describe the relationships.

Vocabulary/Term Tracker

Information Literacy Standards for Student Learning: 1, 2, 3, 4, 6

NCTE/IRA Standards for the English Language Arts: 1, 3, 4, 5, 6, 11, 12

Students will encounter many unfamiliar words while reading the text. There are some terms that students will need to learn so that comprehension is achieved. Additionally, students will stumble upon terms that they find interesting or intriguing. Have students use the Term Tracker in Figure 7.1 to keep a record of their assigned and self-selected vocabulary. Students write the term, their self-created definition using context clues, the definition from a source such as a dictionary, and the page number on which they found the term. The following terms can be used:

1. stalwart
2. agape
3. monosyllabic
4. admonish
5. sentinel
6. raucous
7. tarpaulin
6. tumultuous
9. pallbearer
10. segregation
11. advocate
12. swath
13. chastise
14. chagrin
15. bemuse
16. acquiesce
17. asunder
18. errant

In addition to the already listed words, the classroom teacher or librarian should allow students to self-select terms. In essence, the Term Tracker is an individual dictionary page.

Figure 7.1: Term Tracker

Term Tracker

Name: _____

Vocabulary Term	Self-Created Definition	Definition from Source	Page Number

Role Play: Mississippi 1941

Information Literacy Standards for Student Learning: 1, 2, 3, 4, 5, 6, 7, 8, 9

NCTE/IRA Standards for the English Language Arts: 1, 3, 5, 6, 9, 11, 12

Create a role play activity for students in order to expose them to the feelings and circumstances that the characters experience in the text. For example, pretend to be an alien from another planet, and ask students to cite reasons they like or do not like the alien. Devise reasons why the alien is good and what he or she brings to them. Then, play devil's advocate and ask students to consider what is wrong with the alien and why they should denounce him or her. Next, have students research Mississippi in 1941 and consider how the role play activity applies to racial situations during that time period. Finally, have students react in their writing journals to the following questions: Have you ever been discriminated against? How did it make you feel? What were the circumstances? For instance, students may have been discriminated against because of age, height or weight. This should give students an understanding of how it feels to be a victim of discrimination. Encourage class discussion and sharing of ideas.

Literacy Strategies for During Reading

Class Discussion Questions/Writing Prompts

Information Literacy Standards for Student Learning: 1, 2, 3, 4, 9

NCTE/IRA Standards for the English Language Arts: 1, 2, 4, 6, 9, 10, 11, 12

The following questions can be used as writing prompts and class discussion questions:

1. What are Clarence's and Moe's reasons for joining the army? Are these reasons justified? Why or why not? What are other reasons men and women join the army or other armed forces?

2. When Statler, Troy, and Leon are in the woods, what did you predict would happen? Was your prediction correct or incorrect? If you were the author, what might you change or do differently?

3. What were Sissy's intentions for saying that Clarence was not the father of her child? Did you agree or disagree with her?

4. Describe the relationship between Sissy and Harris.

5. Describe the relationship between Stacey and Cassie. How does it change doing the course of the book? What elements of their relationship stay the same? Can you relate to this relationship? If so, explain in detail.

6. Describe Mr. Jamison's role in the book. Do you think he is aware of how Statler and Troy treat the boys and Cassie?

7. Why do you think Moe finally decided to rebel against Statler and his brothers? Would you have done the same? What might you do differently?

8. Why do you think Jeremy never told on Moe? Would you have made the same decision?

Question-Answer Relationships

Information Literacy Standards for Student Learning: 1, 2, 3, 4, 6, 7

NCTE/IRA Standards for the English Language Arts: 1, 3, 5, 6, 11, 12

The Question-Answer Relationship (QAR) strategy, developed by Taffy Raphael, is a student-centered questioning technique that teaches readers to categorize questions according to where they would find the answers in text. QAR gives students and teachers a common language to use. QAR requires teachers to explicitly model the types of questions typically asked by teachers and tests; even standardized test questions (Raphael and Au 2005). QAR relationships consist of four types of questions: *Right There*, *Think and Search*, *Author and You*, and *On Your Own* (Raphael 1982, 1984, 1986). Require students to use the QAR Worksheet found in Figure 7.2 to create questions for each chapter. These questions can be used in discussion groups or whole class discussions throughout the reading of text. Furthermore, requiring students to create their own questions about the reading enables students to think more deeply about the text and relate it to their own experiences.

Question Answer Relationship

In the Text Questions	In My Head Questions
Right There	Author and You
Think and Search	On My Own

Post-Reading Activities

Chapter Mapping

Information Literacy Standards for Student Learning: 1, 2, 3, 4, 6, 7, 8, 9

NCTE/IRA Standards for the English Language Arts: 1, 3, 4, 5, 6, 8, 11, 12

Have students choose a chapter from the book and create a story map using a word processing program, Inspiration©, or Kidspiration©. The alternative is to assign chapters to students. Ensure students create a visual representation and include the setting, characters, sequence of events or plot development, conflict or problem, and resolution for the assigned chapter. Use the Chapter Map Rubric in Figure 7.3 for assessment purposes. Figure 7.4 is an example of a chapter map. Have students make enough copies of their chapter map for the group. Allow the creator of the map to dictate the correct answers. Guide students through this process, ensuring that all students understand that there is sometimes more than one answer to the same question.

Chapter Map Rubric

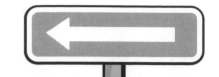

Criteria	Exemplary (3)	Satisfactory (2)	Unsatisfactory (1)
Map	Includes all literary elements (setting, characters, problem, solution, etc.)		Does not include all literary elements (setting, characters, problem, solution, etc.)
Mechanics	There are 0-1 errors in capitalization, punctuation, and/or grammar.	There are 2-3 errors in capitalization, punctuation, and/or grammar.	There are 4 or more errors in capitalization, punctuation, and/or grammar.
Use of Technology	Use of technology is superior and is visually appealing to reader. It is apparent that the student dedicated much time and effort to the project.	Use of technology is satisfactory and is somewhat visually appealing to reader.	Use of technology is unsatisfactory and is visually unappealing to reader. It is apparent that the student did not dedicate time and effort to the project.

Figure 7.4: Chapter Map Example

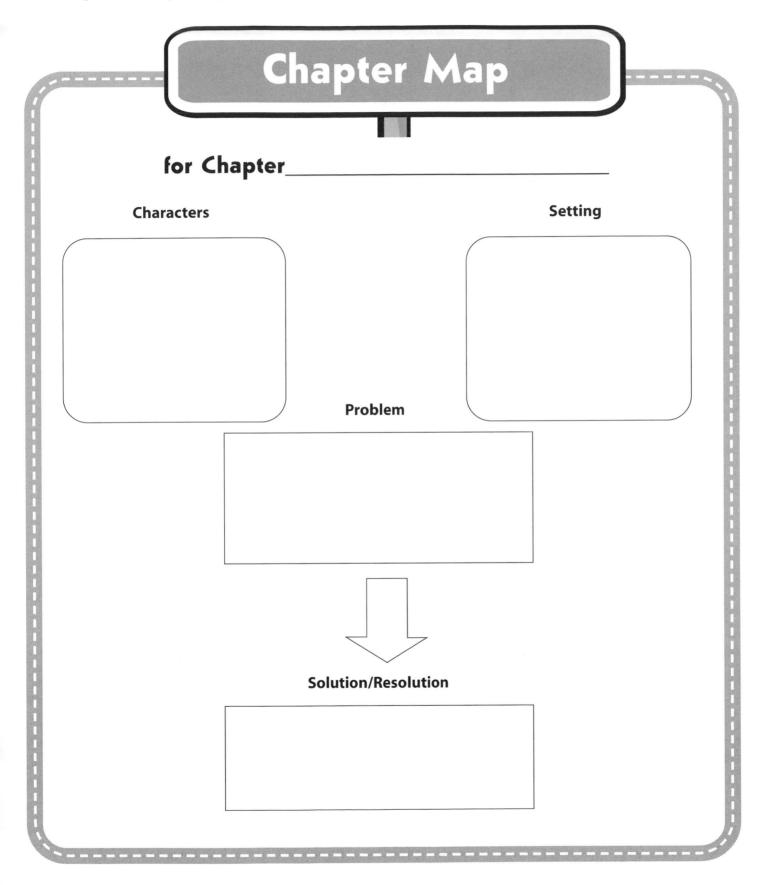

Author Information Brochure/Booktalk

Information Literacy Standards for Student Learning: 1, 2, 3, 4, 5, 6, 7, 8, 9

NCTE/IRA Standards for the English Language Arts: 1, 3, 4, 5, 6, 7, 8, 9, 11, 12

Students will choose an author and develop a brochure highlighting the author's work and life. Have students gather information from the Internet in reference to their selected author. Require students to include the following information in their brochure: brief biography of author's life, titles written by author, picture of author (if applicable), quotes by author, and any additional information the students would like to include. The Author Information Brochure Rubric in Figure 7.5 can be used for assessment purposes. Once students create their brochures, have them develop a booktalk. "Booktalks serve to 'hook' students into reading the text" (Bernadowski, 2008, p. 28). By providing provocative and exciting portions of text to share with classmates, students can potentially increase circulation of certain texts. Limit booktalks to 10 minutes per student. Students should include titles from their Author Information Brochure, and those titles should serve as the focal point of the book talk. Use the Booktalk Grader in Figure 7.6 for guidelines and assessment. Students can use this prior to speaking to self-assess their preparation.

Figure 7.5: Author Information Brochure Rubric

Name:_____

Date:_____

Levels of Performance

(Level of performance and points earned for this assignment are circled for each performance indicator.)

Performance Indicators	Outstanding (10)	Competent (8)	Satisfactory (6)	Poor (4)	Unacceptable (2)
Biography of Author's Life	Contains a biography of the author's life in a highly detailed, very well-written manner.	Contains a biography of the author's life in a detailed and well-written manner.	Contains a biography of the author's life in a somewhat detailed and well-written manner.	Lacks adequate detail about the author's life. Written description is poor.	Written description is unacceptable or missing.
Titles Written by Author	Contains an extensive list of titles written by the author.	Contains an adequate list of titles written by the author.	Contains a somewhat adequate list of titles written by the author.	Contains inadequate list of titles written by the author.	Does not contain a list of titles written by the author.
Quotes by Author	Contains interesting and intriguing quotes by the author with extensive citations.	Contains interesting and intriguing quotes by the author with appropriate citations.	Contains somewhat interesting quotes by the author with citations.		Does not contains quotes by the author.
Layout and Design	Layout and design was exceptional. There was sufficient white space and the designer considered the reader in the development of brochure.	Layout and design was good. There was sufficient white space and the designer considered the reader in the development of brochure.	Layout and design was satisfactory. There was sufficient white space.	Layout and design was unsatisfactory. There was insufficient white space and the designer did not consider the reader in the development of brochure.	Layout and design was unacceptable.
Mechanics and Usage	Plans have 0-3 errors in spelling, capitalization, punctuation, sentence structure, paragraphing, and/or subject-verb agreement.	Plans have 4-5 errors in spelling, capitalization, punctuation, sentence structure, paragraphing, and/or subject-verb agreement.	Plans have 6-7 errors in spelling, capitalization, punctuation, sentence structure, paragraphing, and/or subject-verb agreement.	Plans have 8-9 errors in spelling, capitalization, punctuation, sentence structure, paragraphing, and/or subject-verb agreement.	Plans have 10 or more errors in spelling, capitalization, punctuation, sentence structure, paragraphing, and/or subject-verb agreement.
Professional Presentation	Professional quality was outstanding. Brochure was highly organized and highly professional in appearance.	Professional quality was good. Brochure was organized and professional in appearance.	Professional quality was satisfactory. Brochure was somewhat organized and professional in appearance.	Professional quality was poor. Brochure was disorganized or unprofessional in appearance.	Professional quality was unacceptable. Brochure was very disorganized and unprofessional in appearance.

Total Points: _____ / 100

Figure 7.6: Booktalk Grader

Book Talk Grader

Name(s):_____

Title of Books:_____

Performance Indicator	Point Value Awarded (2 points each)
CONTENT	
My topic and resources were suitable for my audience.	/(2)
The examples I used in my talk were interesting to audience and complemented my subject/theme.	/(2)
ORGANIZATION	
I organized idea(s) and content logically.	/(2)
I made smooth transitions from item to item that linked them together.	/(2)
My talk flowed smoothly.	/(2)
ORAL PRESENTATION	
I kept within the 10-minute time frame.	/(2)
I used an effective opening to catch the attention of my audience.	/(2)
I used vocal variety and emphasis; I paced my speed (not too fast/too slow).	/(2)
I made constant eye contact with audience. I did not consult my notes often.	/(2)
I did not display nervous mannerisms.	/(2)
I expressed interest and enthusiasm and my enjoyment was evident to my audience.	/(2)

Additional Information about the Author

Mildred Taylor is a former Peace Corp volunteer, English teacher, and author of many highly acclaimed books. She has written many books including *Song of the Trees, Roll of Thunder, Hear My Cry, Let the Circle Be Unbroken, The Friendship,* and *Mississippi Bridge.* She has won many awards including the Council on Interracial Books Award, *Times* Outstanding Book of the Year, ALAN Award, and the Coretta Scott King Award.

Additional Resources

Electronic Resources

Nossiter, A. (May 8, 2007). 50 Years Later, Little Rock Can't Escape Race. In *New York Times*. Retrieved October 14, 2008 from <www.newyorktimes.com>.

> The article discusses the epic desegregation at Central High School in Little Rock, Arkansas.

Trueman, C. (2000). *History Learning Site*. In John Kennedy and Civil Rights. Retrieved October 14, 2008, from <http://www.historylearningsite.co.uk/john_kennedy_and_civil_rights.htm2008>.

> The article discusses John Kennedy and Civil Rights Movement during his presidency.

Books

Davis, T. J. (2008). *Race relations in the United States, 1940-1960.* New York: Greenwood Press.

> This comprehensive book about race relations covers two decades. Chapters include Timeline, Overview, Key Events, Voices of the Decade, Race Relations by Group, Law and Government, Media and Mass Communications, Cultural Scene, Influential Theories and Views of Race Relations, and Resource Guide.

Lucas, E. (1997). *Cracking the Wall: The Struggle of the Little Rock Nine.* Minneapolis: Carolrhoda Books.

> An introduction to the nine African-American students who integrated Central High School in Little Rock, Arkansas, in 1957.

Miller, M. (2008). *School Desegregation and the Story of the Little Rock Nine.* New York: Enslow Publishers.

> Additional resource on the Central High School nine.

CHAPTER 8

Toning
the Sweep

Bibliographic Information

Title: *Toning the Sweep*

Author(s): Angela Johnson

Copyright: 1993

Publisher: Scholastic

1994 Coretta Scott King Award Winner

Annotation

Fourteen-year-old Emily and her mother, Diane, go to the desert to help Grandmother Ola pack her house; Grandmother Ola is dying of cancer and cannot stay in her home any longer. As the ladies pack, they learn important lessons about themselves and one another. Emily learns the sacred ritual of "toning the sweep" which is a technique of drumming a plow to make a sound that is a tribute to the dead. This sound was a signal to others in the town that someone had died, and it also served to help the dead person's soul go to heaven. The three strong, independent women's lives intertwine as Emily narrates the story. This story of resilience, self-discovery, and acceptance is compelling for readers, both male and female.

Grade Level: ages 12 and up   **ISBN:** 9780590481427

Discussion Starters/Writing Prompts/Pre-Reading Activities

Journal Writing

Information Literacy Standards for Student Learning: 1, 2, 3, 4, 9

NCTE/IRA Standards for the English Language Arts: 1, 2, 4, 6, 9, 10, 11, 12

Ask students to respond to the following writing prompts in their journals:

1. Predict what the story might be about from the cover of the book. What do you see? What might be implied from the illustration on the cover of the book?

2. Does your family have special rituals in which they engage on a regular basis? If so, explain in detail. What other family rituals do you know of that might be relevant?

3. Describe your relationship with a family member of the same sex. What are some similarities that you share? What are some differences? Has this relationship had obstacles to overcome? If so, give a brief description.

Tragedy Exercise

Information Literacy Standards for Student Learning: 3

NCTE/IRA Standards for the English Language Arts: 3, 4, 9, 11, 12

Require students to complete the Concept Map in Figure 8.1. Students work with a partner to dissect the word *tragedy*. Once students have completed the concept map, allow them to share with the group. Listening to how others define a tragedy based on world and life experiences may prompt students to reexamine their own definition. A class discussion will ensue. A group concept map may help students work on a collaborative definition before, during, and after reading.

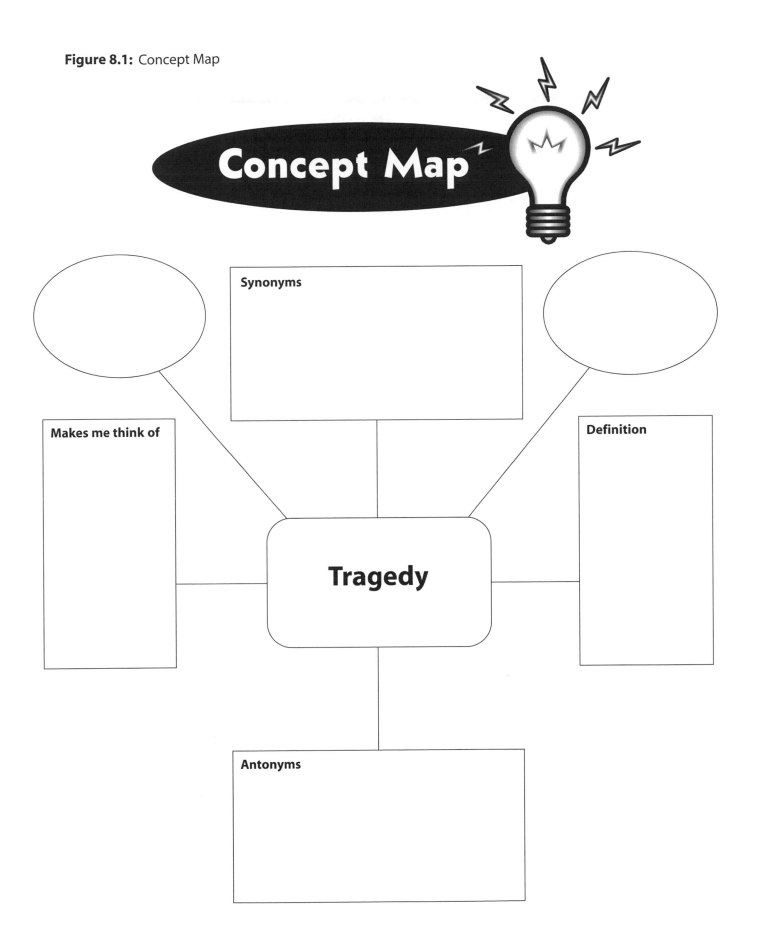

Desert Anticipation Guide

Information Literacy Standards for Student Learning: 1, 2, 3, 4, 5, 6, 7, 8, 9

NCTE/IRA Standards for the English Language Arts: 1, 3, 4, 5, 6, 8, 11, 12

Prior to reading the text, ask students to complete the "before" column of the Desert Anticipation Guide in Figure 8.2. After reading the text, ask students to complete the "after" column on the same Desert Anticipation Guide. Additionally, require students to visit <http://www.livingdesert.org/deserts/default.asp> to read about living in the desert as the characters do in the book. Anticipation Guides can be used to set a purpose for reading, checking and monitoring background knowledge, and checking for comprehension while reading. Students may want to conduct additional research on the topic after reading. Informal assessment of the anticipation guide can be used to measure students' background knowledge as well as what students learned from written and virtual text. Figure 8.3 is the Desert Anticipation Guide Answer Key for the anticipation guide.

Figure 8.2: Desert Anticipation Guide

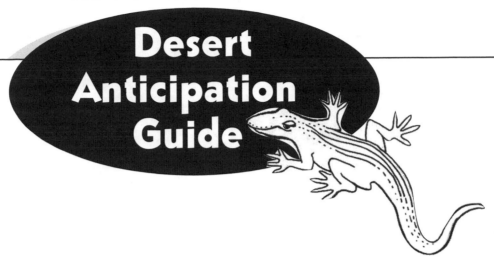

Before

True	False		True	False
		Deserts have little rain; less than 10 inches per year.		
		Many desert animals burrow to find comfort from the high temperature in the desert.		
		There are 14 distinct deserts around the world, at least one in every continent except Europe and Antarctica.		
		Deserts of the world take up about one fourth of the earth's surface.		

After appears above the right True/False columns.

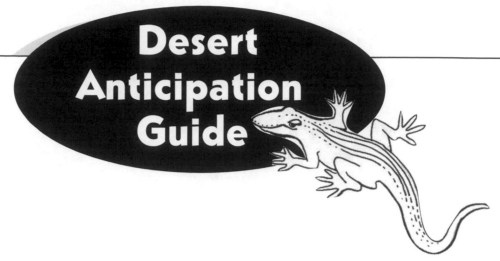

Before   **After**

True	False		True	False
		Deserts have little rain; less than 10 inches per year.	x	
		Many desert animals burrow to find comfort from the high temperature in the desert.	x	
		There are 14 distinct deserts around the world, at least one in every continent except Europe and Antarctica.		X
		Deserts of the world take up about one fourth of the earth's surface.		x

Literacy Strategies for During Reading

Alabama in 1964

Information Literacy Standards for Student Learning: 1, 2, 3

NCTE/IRA Standards for the English Language Arts: 1, 3, 4, 5, 6, 8, 11, 12

While they read the book, require students to research the culture of Alabama in 1964, considering what life was like for African Americans in the South. Have students use multiple sources including books from the library collection, Web sites, and videos. During the book the reader learns that Emily's grandfather was murdered by a white man in 1964 while living in Alabama. Require each student to bring five statements to class about the life for African Americans in Alabama during that time. Write the facts on a large piece of butcher paper and hang it on the wall or bulletin board to use as reference during the reading. Allow students to find themes or ways to categorize the information. Examples of categories include family life, the economy, and society. This will add to students' understanding of Emily's grandmother's attitude about the situation.

Post-Reading Activities

Personal History: A Visual Representation

Information Literacy Standards for Student Learning: 1, 2, 3

NCTE/IRA Standards for the English Language Arts: 1, 3, 4, 5, 6, 8, 11, 12

Emily videotapes much of her grandmother's history through interviews with friends and other acquaintances. Students can opt to make a video or pictorial representation of their own history. If using a video camera, students can conduct interviews to learn about their past and family history or videotape important places or objects by supplying narrative to explain the ideas. If students decide to create a pictorial representation using still photographs, they can take photos and combine the photographs into a photo album with written explanations.

Biography Study

Information Literacy Standards for Student Learning: 1, 2, 3, 4, 5, 6

NCTE/IRA Standards for the English Language Arts: 1, 3, 4, 5, 6, 8, 11, 12

Have students choose a family member or close family friend to be the subject of a biography. Students may want to choose someone they admire or find interesting or intriguing. Students begin this assignment by composing 20 open-ended interview questions. Once questions are created, students make arrangements to interview their biography subject. Students may wish to audio or video tape the interview. Copious note taking is mandatory if relying solely on notes. Next, students will use notes, video, or audio to compose a biography. Finally, encourage students to share their final draft with their biography subject.

Writing Prompts

Information Literacy Standards for Student Learning: 1, 2, 3, 4, 9

NCTE/IRA Standards for the English Language Arts: 1, 2, 4, 6, 9, 10, 11, 12

Use the following questions as writing prompts or book discussion questions:

1. Toning the sweep is a ritual that was once used to help people deal with tragedy, a way to mourn. Discuss ways in which you deal with tragedy or mourn a death.
2. Discuss the dynamic relationship between Diane and her mother.
3. Describe the relationship between Ola and Emily. How is it different or similar to Diane and Ola?
4. Discuss how Emily and Ola feel after leaving the desert for the last time. How would you feel leaving your home?
5. Describe the relationship each woman has to the desert.

Additional Information about the Author

Angela Johnson has many books for young adults with which readers can easily identify. She has also written for young children. Titles include *The Aunt in Our House, Bird, A Cool Midnight,* and *Daddy Calls Me Man.* Johnson attended Kent State University and has worked with Volunteers in Service to America (VISTA), Ravenna, Ohio, as a child development worker, 1981 to 1982; and is currently a freelance writer of children's books.

Additional Resources

Electronic Resources

Mitchell, G. (1999). Care Givers. Retrieved October 14, 2008, from <www.care-givers.com>.

This Web site includes many resources for children and adults who are dealing with grief. Resources include book titles, articles, hyperlinks to other sites, and activities.

Arizona Office of Tourism. (2008). <www.arizonaguide.com>. In *Arizona Guide*, 2008. Retrieved October 14, 2008 from <www.arizonaguide.com>.

The official Web site of the state of Arizona. Provides readers with everything from where to stay, where to go, and what to do. Students can use this site to research Arizona, the setting of *Toning the Sweep.*

Books

Abelove, J. (1999). *Saying It Out Loud.* New York: DK Publishers.

Sixteen-year-old Mindy sorts through her relationships with her mother and father as she tries to come to terms with the fact that her mother is dying from a brain tumor.

Albom, M. (1997). *Tuesdays with Morrie*. New York: Doubleday.

> The story of a young man and his dying mentor. The book chronicles their conversations about life, death, and everything in between.

Aliki. (1987). *The Two of Them*. New York: HarperTrophy.

> A story book that explores death of a grandparent and the relationship between a grandfather and granddaughter.

Blume, J. (1991). *Tiger Eyes*. New York: Bantam Doubleday Dell Books for Young Readers.

> Davey Wexler recovers from the shock of her father's death during a holdup of his 7-Eleven store in Atlantic City.

Kadohta, C. (2004). *Kira-Kira*. New York: Atheneum.

> This Japanese-American story tells the loss of an older sister who dies of lymphoma. This book won a Newbery Award and a Pennsylvania School Librarians Best of the Best Children's Books Choice Award.

CHAPTER 9

Bibliographic Information

Title: *Slam!*

Author(s): Walter Dean Myers

Copyright: 1996

Publisher: Scholastic

1997 Coretta Scott King Award Winner

Annotation

Slam! is about an African-American teenage athlete named Greg, a.k.a. Slam. Greg is a high school student and a star basketball player who lives in the ghettos of New York with his younger brother and mother. The struggles of living in the ghetto, succeeding in school, dealing with peers and peer pressure, and maintaining a relationship with his girlfriend is the center-piece of the story.

Grade Level: ages 12 and up   **ISBN:** 9780545055741

Discussion Starters/Writing Prompts/Pre-Reading Activities

Prior to Reading Discussion

Information Literacy Standards for Student Learning: 1, 9

NCTE/IRA Standards for the English Language Arts: 4, 9, 11, 12

Prior to reading the text, ask students to write about their dreams and aspirations. What do they plan to do in their future? How far will they go to achieve their goals and dreams? Are their dreams realistic in today's society?

Dream Job Research

Information Literacy Standards for Student Learning: 1, 2, 3, 9

NCTE/IRA Standards for the English Language Arts: 1, 3, 4, 5, 6, 7, 8, 11, 12

Ask students to research their dream job or occupation. What salary is average for the geographic location in which they want to live? What are the job requirements? What are the educational requirements? If college is required, how many years and what institutions offer such programs? Students will spend time using the Internet to essentially map their future and the possibilities. If their dream jobs are out of reach for financial reasons, ask them to explore their second choice. Job sites such as <www.monster.com> or <ww.bls.goc/OCO/> are two places to begin this research.

Tour of Harlem

Information Literacy Standards for Student Learning: 1, 2, 3, 9

NCTE/IRA Standards for the English Language Arts: 1, 3, 4, 5, 6, 7, 8, 11, 12

Have students visit <http://www.columbia.edu/cu/iraas/harlem/> to investigate Harlem. Divide the class into three groups. Each group is responsible for a different element of Harlem. Group one will research arts and culture, group two will explore the ethnicity of the city, and group three will be responsible for politics. After visiting the above Web site, students explore each area and collect 10 facts about their element of Harlem. The students then return to the class to share their information. Students can create PowerPoint® presentations to share with the class.

Literature Circles

Information Literacy Standards for Student Learning: 1, 2, 3, 5, 9

NCTE/IRA Standards for the English Language Arts: 1, 2, 3, 4, 5, 6, 9, 10, 11, 12

Prior to students reading the book, assign them to literature circles. When reading in class or during book club time, students meet with their individual groups to discuss their reading. Each group should have six students because each student is responsible for one of six jobs. The job titles include Discussion Starter, Illustrator/Visual Literacy, Word Wizard/Vocabulary Enhancer, Passage Picker, Summarizer, and Connector. Each job is described in Figure 9.1 Literature Circle Jobs. This handout can be distributed to students so they are fully aware of their responsibility during the discussion time. Each student is responsible for their assigned job during each reading session, and they must be fully prepared when they come to the literature discussion to do their job to the best of their ability. Students should rotate jobs so that each student in the group has a chance to experience each job throughout the reading of the book. Accountability is essential so that each discussion group has a focus and direction. No student should be sitting quietly during discussion time. The discussion group is a time to reflect, connect, and interact with co-readers. Use this format throughout the reading of the book.

Job #1: Discussion Starter Your job is to begin the discussion. You are the first person to speak. Prepare questions prior to meeting and be sure to include everyone in the group. Read and discuss all of your quesitons. Develop questions that lead to discussion, such as open-ended questions.

Job #2: Illustrator/Visual Literacy Your job is to make the reading come to life in a visual manner by showing a picture, illustrating a chapter or chapters, using a graphic organizer to organize information in a chapter or chapters, story map or other visual strategy. Ask group members to describe how they would have illustrated the reading.

Job #3: Word Wizard/Vocabulary Enhancer Your job is to find vocabulary that you found interesting, odd or unknown. You read your word and the page number and the other group members use context clues to figure out the meaning. If no context can be used to generate a definition, ask group members to take a guess. Then, provide the definiton. Encourage group members to identify other words that you may not have covered.

Job #4: Passage Picker Your job is to find interesting or intriguing passages in the text to share with the group. Instruct all group members to turn to the page as you read it aloud. Then, ask members to react to the passage. Allow each member a time to share their thoughts. Prompt other members to share their favorite passages.

Job #5: Summarizer Your job is to summarize the text that was read in your own words. Ask members to add additional details if necessary.

Job #6: Connector Your job is to share several connections you made with the text. Allow group members to ask you questions or add their thoughts. You can make text-to-text, text-to-self, and text-to-world connections. Be sure to identify each by name.

Literacy Strategies for During Reading

Character Change

Information Literacy Standards for Student Learning: 1, 2, 3, 9

NCTE/IRA Standards for the English Language Arts: 1, 3, 4, 9, 10, 11, 12

Require students to fold an 8 1/2 x 11 piece of paper, making two columns. Column one is labeled page number and column two is labeled change. Each time students encounter an internal or personal change in Greg (Slam) in the book, have them document the page number and a description of the change that takes place in Greg. Ask students to share periodically with the class both the change and the page number. Students can read the passages aloud.

Discussion Questions

Information Literacy Standards for Student Learning: 1, 2, 3, 4, 9

NCTE/IRA Standards for the English Language Arts: 1, 2, 4, 6, 9, 10, 11, 12

Use the following for discussion questions or writing prompts:

1. Discuss Slam's strengths and weaknesses. Can you relate to one of his strengths? Explain. Can you relate to one of his weaknesses? Explain.

2. Describe the relationship between Mtishia and Slam. How does the relationship change over time? Stay the same?

3. Discuss the transformation of Ice. How would you handle the situation? What would you do the same as Slam? Differently?

4. Predict what Slam does five years from the present. Will he be playing professional ball, attending college, or working for a living? Explore the possibilities.

5. If you suspected a friend was dealing drugs, what would you do? Explain in detail.

6. Describe how people around "Slam" are stereotyping him. How does he or doesn't he live up to those stereotypes?

7. How is Slam's struggle similar to teens living in today's world? Does Myers accurately depict this teen in your opinion?

8. Discuss how Slam's relationship with his grandmother affects his life both positively and negatively.

9. Slam confronts his friend who is slipping into the world of drugs. Would you have the courage to do the same? What would you do differently than Slam?

10. Slam struggles to excel academically. Discuss how this pressure can affect your life as a teenager.

11. Discuss the pros and cons of being a teen athlete.

Post-Reading Activities

Writing an Afterward

Information Literacy Standards for Student Learning: 4, 5, 6

NCTE/IRA Standards for the English Language Arts: 1, 3, 4, 5, 6, 9, 11, 12

Require students to write an afterward of the book. The afterward can take place five, 10 or 15 years from the original setting. Encourage students to write similar to Walter Dean Myers in order to make the afterward fully believable.

Book Review

Information Literacy Standards for Student Learning: 1, 2, 3, 4, 5, 6, 8, 9

NCTE/IRA Standards for the English Language Arts: 1, 3, 4, 5, 6, 9, 11, 12

Have students write a book review to post on *TeenInk Magazine's* Web site at <http://www.teenink.com>, which allows students to publish book reviews online. Students can submit written work, illustrations, or photographs. Take time to review submission guidelines with students. Additionally, ensure students have several people check their work for proper grammar, punctuation, and spelling. If students' work is published, they receive a copy of the magazine and a few small gifts. Students will enjoy seeing their name in print.

Annotations Compilation

Information Literacy Standards for Student Learning: 1, 2, 3, 4, 5, 6, 7, 8, 9

NCTE/IRA Standards for the English Language Arts: 1, 3, 4, 5, 6, 9, 11, 12

Have students compile a list with annotations of young adult fiction that deals with athletics. Students can use a variety of sources to find 10 books that relate to athletics that would be of interest to teens. Students should include the title of the book, author, ISBN number, reading level, and a brief annotation in their own words. Each list should be typed in a word processing program ensuring correct use of mechanics. The library media specialist or classroom teacher can make copies of each list and distribute to students who are interested in such titles. Use the Annotation Compilation Rubric in Figure 9.2 as an assessment tool.

Additional Information about the Author

Walter Dean Myers has written many books for teens. His most recent publications include *Shooter* (2004), *I've Seen the Promised Land: Martin Luther King* (2004), *Constellation* (2004), *Antarctica* (2004), *Here in Harlem: Poems in Many Voices* (2004), *Autobiography of My Dead Brother* (2005) and *Hellfighters: When Pride Met Courage* (2006).

Figure 9.2: Annotation Compilation Rubric

Name: _____

Annotation Compilation Rubric

Criteria	2	1	0
Title/Author	Each annotation includes title and author.	One annotation is missing title and/or author.	Two or more annotations are missing titles and/or authors.
ISBN/Reading Level	Each annotation includes both the ISBN number and the reading level.	One annotation is missing ISBN number and/or the reading level.	Two or more annotations are missing ISBN numbers and/or the reading levels.
Annotations	Each title includes a comprehensive annotation that is well-written.	Each title includes an annotation.	Each title does not include an annotation.
Presentation of Paper	The list is typed using at least 12 point font and formatted in a way that is easy to read.		The list is either not typed or it is not easy to read.
Mechanics	There are 0-2 errors in capitalization, punctuation, and/or grammar.	There are 3-5 errors in capitalization, punctuation, and/or grammar.	There are 6 or more errors in capitalization, punctuation, and/or grammar.

Additional Resources

Electronic Resources

Chevalier, P.J. (2001). On drugs in sports. *The Sporting News.* 225-32.

A brief article about the use of drugs in sports that can be a valuable extension of the book's topic.

Hurston, Z. N. (2007). In African-American Literature Book Club 2007. Retrieved October 20, 2008 from <http:aalbc.com/authors/harlemslang.htm>.

This Web site has a list of many slang terms used in Harlem and definitions of the terms.

Books

Panpel, F.C. (2007). *Drugs and Sports.* New York: Facts on File.

This book explores the world of drugs and sports in which many athletes find themselves involved.

CHAPTER 10

Bibliographic Information

Title: *Heaven*

Author(s): Angela Johnson

Copyright: 1998

Publisher: Scholastic

1999 Coretta Scott King Award Winner

Annotation

Fourteen-year-old Marley's life in the small town of Heaven is disrupted when she discovers that her father and mother are not her real parents. The book follows the life of a teenager and the heartaches and triumphs of a teen living a lie.

Grade Level: Young Adult   **ISBN:** 9780689822902

Discussion Starters/Writing Prompts/Pre-Reading Activities

Questions to Ponder

Information Literacy Standards for Student Learning: 1, 2, 3, 4, 9

NCTE/IRA Standards for the English Language Arts: 1, 2, 4, 6, 9, 10, 11, 12

Use the following as writing prompts or pre-reading discussion questions:

1. In what ways does our past affect our future? Use an example from your own life to support your answer.

2. Look at the cover of the book. Predict what you think the book might be about from the illustration and title.

3. What insights do you think dreams give us into our subconscious? Can you give an example of a dream that might tell us something about you?

Comparing Three Sources/The 1963 Birmingham Bombing

Information Literacy Standards for Student Learning: 1, 2, 3, 4, 5, 6, 7, 8, 9

NCTE/IRA Standards for the English Language Arts: 1, 2, 3, 4, 5, 6, 7, 8, 9, 11, 12

Heaven takes place in the summer of 1996 when many southern black churches were being burned, which reminds Marley's parents of the 1960s. In order for students to understand the complexity and severity of these tragedies, require students to investigate the Birmingham Church Bombing of 1963. Using the Comparison Chart in Figure 10.1 ask students to read three different sources on the topic. Use the following sources or choose others:

* <http://www.english.uiuc.edu/maps/poets/m_r/randall/birmingham.htm>
* Weatherford, Carole Boston. *Birmingham 1963*. Boyds Mills Press, 1993.
* *4 Little Girls*. Dir. Spike Lee. Dianne Braddock, 1997.

Figure 10.1: Comparison Chart

Comparison Chart

Source 1	Source 2	Source 3

Researching Names

Information Literacy Standards for Student Learning: 1, 7, 8, 9

NCTE/IRA Standards for the English Language Arts: 1, 3, 5, 6, 8, 11, 12

The main character in *Heaven* is named Marley after the late Jamaican singer, Bob Marley. Require students to research their names by interviewing parents and grandparents. Students will bring their information back to the group and share their stories. Prompt students who are named after a relative to share a story about that relative and why their parents chose to name them after that particular person.

Literacy Strategies for During Reading

Dream Detectives

Information Literacy Standards for Student Learning: 1, 7, 8, 9

NCTE/IRA Standards for the English Language Arts: 1, 3, 7, 8, 9, 11, 12

While reading the book, require students to keep a dream journal. At the end of each week ask students to bring their dream journals to class to share with classmates. The following Web site is a helpful place to start to begin an analysis of dreams: <http://www.dreammoods.com/dreamdictionary>.

Timely Music

Information Literacy Standards for Student Learning: 1, 4, 9

NCTE/IRA Standards for the English Language Arts: 11, 12

Marley was named after Bob Marley who was extremely influential as a singer. Choose songs by Bob Marley to share with the class. Begin a discussion about why his music was influential. What stories do some of his lyrics tell? Allow students to share some of their influential musicians and answer the same question.

Post-Reading Activities

Writing to Relatives

Information Literacy Standards for Student Learning: 1, 2, 3, 4, 5, 6

NCTE/IRA Standards for the English Language Arts: 1, 2, 3, 4, 5, 6, 9, 11, 12

Jack, who Marley believes is her uncle at the beginning of the story, writes fascinating notes to her about his travels. Have students find a far-off relative with whom to communicate through writing. Ask students to describe themselves today, and what they have been doing since they last saw or talked to the relative. Students should also describe their family, friends, and school life. An alternative is to allow students to "act" as a far-off relative and write as pen pals.

Secrets

Information Literacy Standards for Student Learning: 1, 9

NCTE/IRA Standards for the English Language Arts: 11, 12

Everyone has secrets. Marley's parents had a big secret and eventually she finds out the truth. Give each student two small pieces of paper and require them to write two secrets on the paper without anyone seeing what they are writing. They should do this quietly since others will eventually have to guess their secret. Ask students to write one secret of their own and on the other paper write a secret they have kept. If students feel uncomfortable sharing intimate thoughts, allow them to write fake secrets. Fold all papers and put in a hat or cup. Shake up the papers and allow students to pick one and read it aloud. Students discuss why this would be an easy or difficult secret to keep and the consequences, if any, of keeping the secret. Discuss why it is sometimes important to tell one's secret such as when it risks their lives or endangers others. When the game is complete, the teacher or library media specialist shares with students a secret they told because it was the right thing to do, and asks students what they would have done the same or differently.

Comic Strip

Information Literacy Standards for Student Learning: 1, 9

NCTE/IRA Standards for the English Language Arts: 4, 9, 11, 12

Have students create a comic strip that represents a scene in the book. Students can illustrate the comic strip themselves or create a comic strip at <readwritethink.org/materials/comic> and print after completion.

Additional Information about the Author

Angela Johnson was born June 18, 1961 in Tuskegee, Alabama, attended Kent State University, and currently works as a freelance writer. Her titles include The First Part Last, Heaven, The Other Side: Shorter Poems, and When I Was Old. Many of her titles have been awarded the Coretta Scott King medal.

Additional Resources

Electronic Resources

Brennan, C. (2007). The other mother: out of the blue, her grown daughter announced that she'd tracked down her birth mother—and that she was coming to dinner soon. Carol Brennan on the crazy quilt of emotions when mom meets mom. (adoption). *O, The Oprah Magazine, 8*(4), 219.

This article explores the world of adoption when children grow up and search for their birth mothers.

Messer, L. (2008). A second chance at love. *People Weekly, 70*(14), 133.

> A gentle story of adoption.

Books

BuckingHam, R. W. (1997). *I'm Pregnant, Now What Do I Do?* New York: Prometheus.

> This book explores the choices that women have when they become pregnant, including adoption.

Crutcher, C. (2001). *Whale Talk*. New York: Dell.

> The story of a boy whose mother abandons him when she becomes involved in drugs.

Lowry, L. (1978). *Find a Stranger Say Goodbye*. New York: Bantam.

> A story for young adults about the issue of saying goodbye to a birth mother.

Slade, S. (2007). *Adopted: The Teens Ultimate Guide*. New York: Scarecrow.

> A guidebook for teens that are adopted and need some insights.

CHAPTER 11

The First Part Last

Bibliographic Information

Title: *The First Part Last*

Author(s): Angela Johnson

Copyright: 2003

Publisher: Simon & Schuster

2004 Coretta Scott King Award Winner

Annotation

The short narrative tells the story of 16-year-old Bobby and his infant daughter Feather. The narrative is told in alternating chapters between "Then" (the day Bobby found out his girlfriend was pregnant and what followed) and "Now" (Bobby's struggles as a single parent in high school). The mystery of why Bobby is a single parent, why he kept the baby against his parents' wishes, and where Feather's mother is slowly unravels as the "Then" and "Now" story-lines intersect and intertwine.

Grade Level: Young Adult   **ISBN:** 0689849230

Discussion Starters/Writing Prompts/Pre-Reading Activities

Parent Interview

Information Literacy Standards for Student Learning: 1, 3

NCTE/IRA Standards for the English Language Arts: 4, 7, 11, 12

Before students read the text, have them arrange to interview a new parent about their role(s) as a parent. An alternative is to invite a guest speaker to speak to the group. Be sure students ask the new parent how their lives have changed since the birth of their infant. Ask the parent(s) to complete a schedule of their day from the time they wake up until they go to sleep at night. Students then compare that schedule to their own daily schedule. Students should consider the following questions: How do the two schedules differ? What are your reactions to how their day is spent versus how your day is spent? What is the same? Different? What are some conclusions you can make based on this information?

Next, ask students to think about where they want to be in 10 years. Have students make a list of things they will do in 10 years. Finally, ask them to think about how their lives might be different if they suddenly became a parent. Discuss findings with classmates, a literature group or book club.

Literacy Strategies for During Reading

Class Discussion Questions

Information Literacy Standards for Student Learning: 1, 2, 3, 4, 9

NCTE/IRA Standards for the English Language Arts: 1, 2, 4, 6, 9, 10, 11, 12

The following questions can be used for discussion:

1. How does Bobby and Nia's parents react to the news of her pregnancy? Compare their reaction to how you think your parents would react. Is this similar to or different than how you think your parents would react?

2. How would you react if you were a parent of a teen who became pregnant? Is this similar to or different than the characters' parents? Explain.

3. Describe Bobby at the beginning of the book. Find a quote that best describes him in the beginning. Then, describe Bobby at the end of the book. Find a quote that best describes him at the end of the book. How does he stay the same? How does he change?

4. How would you cope with the circumstances that Bobby finds himself? How is his reaction different from or the same as your own reaction might be? Explain your answer in detail.

5. How do you think the dynamic between Bobby and Feather might be different if Nia helped raise Feather? How would it be the same?

6. Describe your feelings towards Mary and Fred. Do you agree or disagree with their grand- parenting? Explain what you can agree with and with what you cannot agree. How do you think your parents would act? Similar to? Different than?

7. What would you tell Nia about her family if you had the chance? What would you purposely leave out of the conversation and why?

8. What is the significance of the title? Why do you think Angela Johnson chose this title? What would you title this book?

9. How would this story differ if Mia and Bobby were raising Feather together as a family?

10. Do you think being a teen parent is easier or harder for males? Explain your answer in detail.

Finding Conflict

Information Literacy Standards for Student Learning: 1, 2

NCTE/IRA Standards for the English Language Arts: 1, 3, 4, 5, 6, 11, 12

Bobby faces many challenges throughout the text. Have students keep a Character Conflict Chart Record of when the main character is faced with a conflict (chapter and page number), the type of conflict he faces (internal, external, and so on) and how he deals with the conflict. Then, require students to write how this conflict changes Bobby. Students can keep the chart in their reading logs or diaries. The Character Conflict Chart Record can be found in Figure 11.1.

Character Conflict Chart Record

Name: _____

Conflict	Chapter	Page Number	Type of Conflict	The character deals with the conflict by . . .	In what ways is the character changed?

Making a Connection/Class Chain Link

Information Literacy Standards for Student Learning: 1, 2

NCTE/IRA Standards for the English Language Arts: 1, 3, 4, 5, 6, 11, 12

As students read a text, it is important that they make connections to what they are reading.

Make sure students have opportunities to discuss how they may be connecting with the text. Teach students to identify their connections in one of three ways: Text-to-Self, Text-to-Text, or Text-to-World. Make a class paper chain of page numbers and quotes that students find they have connected with in some way. Encourage students to use Post-it Notes© to keep track of when they connected and how they felt so they can share that in class or book club. Once they have shared their connection(s), encourage them to write the information on a piece of construction paper, connect, and staple it to the class chain link.

Vocabulary Word Bank

Information Literacy Standards for Student Learning: 1, 2

NCTE/IRA Standards for the English Language Arts: 1, 3, 4, 5, 6, 11, 12

While reading the text, students may encounter unfamiliar words as they read. Give each student a blank sheet of paper (8 1/2 x 11) and have them fold it into four columns. This will serve as their personal dictionary or word bank while reading the book. In the first column students write the words that they encounter. In the second column students write the context of the word, including all words surrounding the unfamiliar word that might be helpful in determining its definition (context clues). In the third column, students take a guess at the meaning based on the context from the book and write it in column two. Finally, students ask a peer or adult what they think the meaning is and write it in column four. Have students bring this Vocabulary Word Bank to class as they are reading the book and share with classmates. During these discussions, students and teachers can discuss the meaning of the words. Students can then make modifications to their own meanings if needed.

Post-Reading Activities

Database

Information Literacy Standards for Student Learning: 1, 2, 3, 6, 7, 8, 9

NCTE/IRA Standards for the English Language Arts: 1, 3, 4, 5, 6, 11, 12

With a partner or group, have students create a database of resources that would be useful on the topic of teen pregnancy or other teen issues related to the book. Require students to list the location of the resource, cost (if any), and a description or summary of the information. Students can use the Internet to collect information. The teacher or library media specialist will compile the databases and post the information on the school or library Web site. Share all the database information with the group and encourage students to use the information for personal use.

Writing an Editorial

Information Literacy Standards for Student Learning: 3, 5

NCTE/IRA Standards for the English Language Arts: 1, 3, 4, 5, 6, 11, 12

In this activity, students write an editorial from Bobby's point of view. Using information learned from the text, have students write a hypothetical editorial about teen parenting. Remind students that editorials are persuasive in nature and aim to convince the reader to believe their "side" of an issue. Use the Editorial Rubric in Figure 11.2 to assess students.

Editorial Rubric

Evaluation Criteria	3 (excellent)	2 (average)	1 (poor)
Position/ Persuasive	The paper's position is extremely persuasive/convincing in nature.	The paper's position is somewhat persuasive/convincing in nature.	The paper's position is not persuasive in nature.
Background Information	The editorial contains an abundant amount of background information about the issue in an effort to fully inform the reader.	The editorial contains some background information about the issue in an effort to inform the reader.	The editorial contains very little background information about the issue and/or does not inform the reader.
Lead	The editorial is written with a strong, interesting lead to bring the reader into the story and issue.	The editorial is written with a somewhat interesting/strong lead.	The editorial is written with a weak lead OR no lead is apparent in the editorial.
Support	The article has a clearly stated opinion and contains at least three (3) different, but logical reasons for the stated opinion.	The article has a clearly stated opinion and contains at least two (2) different, but logical reasons for the stated opinion.	The article is either lacking a clearly stated opinion or contains less than two reasons for the stated opinion. The reasons may be illogical.
Transitions	The writer uses transition words effectively between sentences and paragraphs.	The writer uses transition words between sentences and paragraphs in a somewhat effective manner. Some errors exist.	The writer does not use transition words effectively between sentences and paragraphs OR no transitions are used.
Conclusion	The conclusion of the editorial restates all the reasons in one sentence effectively.	The conclusion of the editorial restates most of the reasons in one sentence.	The conclusion of the editorial does not restate the reasons or is not apparent.
Mechanics	There are 0-1 errors in capitalization, punctuation, and/or grammar.	There are 2-3 errors in capitalization, punctuation, and/or grammar.	There are 4 or more errors in capitalization, punctuation, and/or grammar.

Writing a Script

Information Literacy Standards for Student Learning: 3, 5

NCTE/IRA Standards for the English Language Arts: 1, 3, 4, 5, 6, 11, 12

Assign students to work in groups of four or five. Then, assign each group the task of developing a script for television or stage based on a chapter from the book. Once students write the script, they can create props and perform the chapter for the class. This can be done either at the end of the book or groups can perform after each chapter is read. This activity will help students develop a variety of skills such as comprehension, writing, speaking, and listening. Ask the class to write reviews after each group has performed. The Script Writing Rubric in Figure 11.3 can be used for assessment.

Script Writing Rubric

	4	3	2	1
Grammar	Writer makes 1-2 errors in grammar or spelling.	Writer makes 3-4 errors in grammar or spelling.	Writer makes 5-6 errors in grammar or spelling.	Writer makes more than 6 errors in grammar or spelling.
Mechanics	Writer makes 1-2 errors in capitalization and/or punctuation.	Writer makes 3-4 errors in capitalization and/or punctuation.	Writer makes 5-6 errors in capitalization and/or punctuation.	Writer makes more than 6 errors in capitalization and/or punctuation.
Format	The script is written in the correct format. All lines have the correct margin and punctuation.	The script is mostly correct. Either the margin OR punctuation is incorrect.	The script is slightly correct. Both the margins and the punctuation are incorrect.	The script is NOT written in script format.
Content	The story contains many creative details and/or descriptions that contribute to the reader's enjoyment. The author has really used his imagination.	The story contains a few creative details and/or descriptions that contribute to the reader's enjoyment. The author has used his imagination.	The story contains a few creative details and/or descriptions, but they distract from the story. The author has tried to use his imagination.	There is little evidence of creativity in the story. The author does not seem to have used much imagination.
Writing Process	Student devotes a lot of time and effort to the writing process (prewriting, drafting, reviewing, and editing). Works hard to make the story wonderful.	Student devotes sufficient time and effort to the writing process (prewriting, drafting, reviewing, and editing). Works and gets the job done.	Student devotes some time and effort to the writing process but was not very thorough. Does enough to get by.	Student devotes little time and effort to the writing process. Doesn't seem to care.
Professionalism	Script is easy for a reader to understand and follow. It flows and makes sense.	Script has parts that are confusing but the overall intention is clear.	Script is difficult to read and understand. It does not flow. An attempt has been made.	Script does NOT make sense. Reader cannot follow or understand the intention or where the script is going.

Additional Information about the Author

Angela Johnson is a prolific writer for both children and teens. Her latest book *The First Part Last* earned her a Coretta Scott King Award seal as did her 1999 book titled *Heaven*. Her 1998 book of poems titled *The Other Side, The Shorter Poems* earned her a 1999 Coretta Scott King Author Honor Book marking her two honors in the same year, a privilege reserved for only the best. Johnson wrote seven picture books before working up the courage to write her first novel, *Toning the Sweep* (Orchard, 1993), which won the Coretta Scott King Award. During a visit to her brother's house in the California desert, Johnson met some incredible people who became the inspiration for the vibrant characters in *Toning*. Each of Johnson's subsequent novels (*Humming Whispers* [Orchard, 1995] and *Heaven* [Simon & Schuster, 1998]) is set in a place she's visited. Her carefully chosen words in each slim novel convey the depth of her characters and their struggles.

Additional Resources

Electronic Resources

Family First. (2002). *Family Parenting*. In Hands on Parenting. Retrieved October 20, 2008 from <http://www.familyfirst.net/parenting/hands-on.asp>.

Tips for parents on handling many teen issues including teen pregnancy and teen parenting.

Planned Parenthood. (2008). *Pregnancy*. Retrieved on October 17, 2008 from <http://www.plannedparenthood.org/health-topics/pregnancy-4250.htm>.

A resource for teens and their parents on issues such as pregnancy prevention.

Books

Covey, S. (1998). *The 7 Habits of Highly Effective Teens: The Ultimate Teenage Success Guide*. New York: Simon & Schuster.

This book outlines for readers what it takes to be highly effective during the teen years. Students, parents, and teachers would find this an exceptional read.

Mayden, B., W. Castro, & M. Annitto. (1999). *First Talk: A Teen Pregnancy Prevention Dialogue among Latinos*. Washington, DC: CWLA Press.

Published by the Child Welfare League, this book discusses prevention measures taken by the Latino communities to reduce the number of teen pregnancies. This book is also available in Spanish.

Paschal, A. M. (2006). *Voices of African-American Teen Fathers*. New York: Haworth.

Stories of African-American teen fathers are told in this compelling text. Readers encounter firsthand accounts of what it means to be a single male raising a child.

Roles, P. (1990). *Facing Teenage Pregnancy*. Washington, DC: Child Welfare League of America.

Discusses the challenges and obstacles of teen pregnancy.

CHAPTER 12

Bibliographic Information

Title: *Copper Sun*

Author(s): Sharon Draper

Copyright: 2006

Publisher: Simon & Schuster Children's Publishing

2007 Coretta Scott King Award Winner

Annotation

This historical fiction delves into slave trade in the 1700s and follows 15-year-old Amari from sex slave to plantation slave. Readers will find themselves spellbound by the life of this young girl and the horrifying life she is forced to lead. Readers will be surprised by the relationships she develops throughout the text.

Grade Level: Young Adult   **ISBN:** 9781416953487

Discussion Starters/Writing Prompts/Pre-Reading Activities

Slave Research

Information Literacy Standards for Student Learning: 1, 2, 3, 5, 6, 7, 8, 9

NCTE/IRA Standards for the English Language Arts: 1, 3, 4, 5, 6, 11, 12

Before reading the text students will need ample historical preparation to fully comprehend the text and empathize with the main character, Amari. Have students visit <www.sharondraper.com> and visit the "slavery photographs," "account of a slave auction," and "South Carolina and slavery." These three information pieces coupled with additional resources on slave trading will prepare students for the book. Students should write reactions to photographs and narratives in their journals and share with the class during discussion time.

Emancipation Proclamation/Slavery

Information Literacy Standards for Student Learning: 1, 2, 3, 5, 6, 7, 8, 9

NCTE/IRA Standards for the English Language Arts: 1, 3, 4, 5, 6, 11, 12

Require students to write for one minute all they know about the Emancipation Proclamation and Slavery. Students can write anything that comes to mind and it can be in the form of words, phrases, and complete sentences. Allow students time to share what they have written. As students share their thoughts and writing, take notes for the class on the board or butcher paper. Ask each student to write down three things that they are either unsure about or want to learn about the Emancipation Proclamation and slavery. Then group students according to interests. Require students to use many sources to research these ideas. After using a variety of sources, students return to the group and share five things they discovered from their research. All groups should share their information. Finally, ask students to complete a five-minute write where they write everything they now know about the Emancipation Proclamation and slavery.

Literacy Strategies for During Reading

Family Ties

Information Literacy Standards for Student Learning: 1, 2, 3

NCTE/IRA Standards for the English Language Arts: 1, 3, 4, 5, 6, 11, 12

Ask students to think of a family member with whom they are very close and describe the relationship they have with that relative. Make a class list of qualities they possess. Compare the students' descriptions to the relationship between Amari and her relatives. How might you describe Amari's relationship with her parents? Her brother, Kwasi? Besa?

Writing Prompts/Discussion Questions

Information Literacy Standards for Student Learning: 1, 2, 3, 4, 9

NCTE/IRA Standards for the English Language Arts: 1, 2, 4, 6, 9, 10, 11, 12

Use the following questions as discussion starters or writing prompts:

1. Describe the Village of Ziavi. Although physically it differs from your own community, what qualities might be the same? Different?

2. Cite a passage where you relate to Amari. Describe how you relate to her.

3. Describe Mr. and Mrs. Derby. What do you like about each? Dislike?

4. What do Polly and Amari have in common? Describe their relationship from their first meeting until the end of the book. Can you empathize with Polly? Why or why not?

5. Why does Polly begin to treat Amari like an equal? Did you predict this was going to happen?

Character List

Information Literacy Standards for Student Learning: 3

NCTE/IRA Standards for the English Language Arts: 1, 3, 4, 5, 6, 11, 12

Have students use the Character List in Figure 12.1 to document each major and minor character. There are many characters in this book so this handout will help students keep track of them. In addition to the name of the character, students should write three adjectives to describe the character. Allow students to change and adapt adjectives as some characters develop throughout the text.

Character List

Name of Character	Major/Minor	3 Adjectives
1. _____	_____	_____
		_____
		_____
2. _____	_____	_____
		_____
		_____
3. _____	_____	_____
		_____
		_____
4. _____	_____	_____
		_____
		_____
5. _____	_____	_____
		_____
		_____
6. _____	_____	_____
		_____
		_____

Post-Reading Activities

Point of View Correspondence

Information Literacy Standards for Student Learning: 3, 5

NCTE/IRA Standards for the English Language Arts: 1, 3, 4, 5, 6, 11, 12

Have students write a letter from one character's point of view to another character in the book, with a response from that character. For example, a student can write a letter to Amari from Mrs. Derby and then write Amari's reaction to that letter, or write a letter from Besa to Amari and from Amari back to Besa.

Slave Journals

Information Literacy Standards for Student Learning: 3, 5

NCTE/IRA Standards for the English Language Arts: 1, 3, 4, 5, 6, 11, 12

Require students, in groups of three to four, to write a five-day journal from the perspective of a slave. Knowledge gained from pre-reading research and the text will give students adequate knowledge to compose the journal writings. Be sure students are writing the journals in first person and dating the entries accurately. Groups of students then share their journals and decide which group was the most historically accurate and compelling. Record the journals in an MP3 format or allow students to record on Gcast.com. Gcast can be accessed at <http://www.gcast.com/?nr=1&&s=137366802>.

Visual Representation

Information Literacy Standards for Student Learning: 3, 5

NCTE/IRA Standards for the English Language Arts: 1, 3, 4, 5, 6, 11, 12

Ask students to visually represent the most poignant scene in the book. Have each student choose a different scene and represent that scene in some form. The visual representations can be illustrations, video productions, images, clay creations, or any form of visual representation that the student feels comfortable using independently. An alternative is to allow students to work in small groups to create their visual representation. Have students share their creations with the class or write an explanation for others to read. Find a means for displaying the work either electronically or in the library showcase.

Amari's Timeline

Information Literacy Standards for Student Learning: 3, 5

NCTE/IRA Standards for the English Language Arts: 1, 3, 4, 5, 6, 11, 12

In this activity, students create either a visual or written timeline of Amari's journey throughout the book. Although actual dates and times are not readily available, the sequence of events is the key to this activity. Students can create a visual timeline with photographs or illustrations to depict her journey or students can write short descriptions to detail her journey.

Additional Information about the Author

Sharon M. Draper is a former English/Language Arts teacher and an accomplished writer. She has been honored as the National Teacher of the Year, is a five-time winner of the Coretta Scott King Award, and is a *New York Times* bestselling author. Her most recent books for teens include *November Blues* (2007), *Fire from the Rock* (2006) and the *Ziggy* series (2006). Ms. Draper is known for her commitment to education and literacy for children of all ages.

Additional Resources

Electronic Resources

Boston, J. (2006). Sweet Freedom and Its High Price. *U.S. News & World Report.* 3, 42-43.
>   An original slave narrative written by John Boston.

Books

Ennals, J. R. *From Slavery to Citizenship.* John Wiley & Sons: New York, 2007.
>   This book engages readers in considering slavery an issue of present as well as past. Many perspectives are presented in this book about the topic of slavery.

McKissack, Pat. *Days of Jubilee: The End of Slavery in the United States.* Scholastic: New York, 2003.
>   For readers grades five to eight, this book will give students the historical documentation on the gradual end to slavery with an accurate and extensive timeline.

Rappaport, Doreen. *Escape from Slavery: Five Journeys to Freedom.* Harper Trophy: New York, 1991.
>   For readers grades four to seven, this book highlights five stories of slaves and their fight for freedom by means of the Underground Railroad.

Walvin, James. *Black Ivory: Slavery in the British Empire.* Blackwell: Boston, 2001.
>   The story of African slavery and British Colonies in North America.

PART 2

Coretta Scott King Honor Books

Classroom teachers and librarians will find a complete list of the Coretta Scott King Honor Books from the most recent (2008) to the first year an honor book was named (1978) in Figure CSK1. During some years many books were chosen and other years just one honor book was chosen. This comprehensive list can be used as a reference for additional book selections that may be of interest to students. This list can also help develop library or classroom collections. The chart includes the year the book was honored, title of selection, author(s), illustrator (if applicable), recommended age range, publisher/ISBN, and short synopsis. Finally, this list can be distributed to students who want to explore additional texts written by African-American Authors.

Figure CSK2: Coretta Scott King Honor Books

YEAR	TITLE	AUTHOR	RECOMMENDED READING LEVEL	PUBLISHER	ANNOTATION
2009	*The Blacker the Berry*	Joyce Carol Thomas	Ages 4-8	Amistad	A collection of poems celebrating African-American life.
2009	*Keeping the Night Watch*	Hope Anita Smith	Young Adult	Henry Holt and Company	C. J. fights to understand the demise of his own family.
2009	*Becoming Billie Holiday*	Carol Weatherford	Young Adult	Word Song	The legend of Billie Holiday is revealed in this book.
2008	*November Blues*	Sharon M. Draper	Young Adult	Atheneum	November Nelson loses her boyfriend, Josh, but he leaves something important behind that changes her life forever.
2008	*Twelve Rounds to Glory: The Story of Muhammad Ali*	Charles R. Smith Jr., Bryan Collier (Illustrator)	Ages 10 and up	Candlewick Press	A poignant journey of Muhammad Ali's life from childhood to present day.
2007	*The Road to Paris*	Nikki Grimes	Ages 9-12	Putnam Juvenile	Paris, a foster child, tries to find her way in the world as a biracial girl.
2006	*Maritcha: A Nineteenth-Century American Girl*	Tonya Bolden	Ages 5-9	Harry N. Abrams, Inc., Publishers	A memoir of a black girl born free and raised in New York City.
2006	*Dark Sons*	Nikki Grimes	Young Adult	Hyperion Books for Children	Sam feels betrayed by his father who leaves the family to remarry.
2006	*A Wreath for Emmett Till*	Marilyn Nelson, Philippe Lardy (Illustrator)	Ages 12 and up	Houghton Mifflin Company	The true story of a 14-year-old boy who changed the face of the Civil Rights Movement.
2005	*The Legend of Buddy Bush*	Shelia P. Moses	Young Adult	Simon & Schuster Children's	Buddy is jailed for a crime he didn't commit and his family must find a way to set him free.
2005	*Who Am I Without Him?: Short Stories about Girls and the Boys in Their Lives*	Sharon G. Flake	Young Adult	Hyperion	Stories that ring true today about the relationships between teenage boys and girls.
2005	*Fortune's Bones: The Manumission Requiem*	Marilyn Nelson	Young Adult	Boyds Mills Press	A poem written for a slave named Fortune, whose bones are on display at Mattatuck Museum in Waterbury, Connecticut.
2004	*Days of Jubilee: The End of Slavery in the United States*	Patricia C. & Frederick L. McKissack, Leo Dillon (Illustrator)	9 years old	Scholastic	Chronicles the freeing of slaves using sources such as slave narratives, diaries and letters.
2004	*Locomotion*	Jacqueline Woodson	Ages 9-12	Putnam Juvenile	A series of poems written by an 11-year-old boy who lives much of his life in foster care.

YEAR	TITLE	AUTHOR	RECOMMENDED READING LEVEL	PUBLISHER	ANNOTATION
2004	The Battle of Jericho	Sharon Mills Draper	Young Adult	Simon & Schuster Children's	A story about hazing in high schools from a 16-year-old boy's perspective.
2003	The Red Rose Box	Brenda Woods	Ages 8-12	The Putnam Publishing Group	The box holds treasures that help Leah escape from the cotton fields.
2003	Talkin' About Bessie: The Story of Aviator Elizabeth Coleman	Nikki Grimes, E.B. Lewis (Illustrator)	Ages 7-10	Scholastic	The story of the first African-American female pilot told through monologues.
2002	Money-Hungry	Sharon G. Flake	Young Adult	Hyperion Books for Children	Thirteen-year-old Raspberry Hill works to get herself and her mother off the streets.
2002	Carver: A Life in Poems	Marilyn Nelson	Young Adult	Front Street	The book underscores the life of George Washington Carver.
2001	Let It Shine! Stories of Black Women Freedom Fighters	Andrea D. Pinkney, Stephen Alcorn (Illustrator)	Young Adult	Harcourt Children's Books	This book highlights the many triumphs of African-American women in their fight for equal rights.
2000	Francie	Karen English	Ages 12 and up	Farrar, Straus & Giroux	The story of Francie who lives in Alabama and dreams of freedom up North.
2000	Black Hands, White Sails: The Story of African-American Whalers	Patricia C. & Frederick L. McKissack	Ages 12 and up	Scholastic Press	Details the life of African-American whalers from 1730-1880.
2000	Monster	Walter Dean Myers	Young Adult	HarperCollins	Sixteen-year-old Steve Harmon writes about his life in jail and on trail as if it were a movie.
1999	Jazmin's Notebook	Nikki Grimes	Ages 12 and up	Dial Books	Jazmin keeps her memories of growing up in Harlem in the 1960s in a notebook.
1999	Breaking Ground, Breaking Silence: The Story of New York's African Burial Ground	Joyce Hansen, Gary McGowan	Young Adult	Henry Holt and Company	The true story of the burial grounds of African Americans from long ago. The stories of their lives are told by their bones.
1999	The Other Side: Shorter Poems	Angela Johnson	Ages 12 and up	Orchard Books	A collection of poems about growing up black in Alabama.
1998	Bayard Rustin: Behind the Scenes of the Civil Rights Movement	James Haskins	Ages 10 and up	Hyperion	The story of Civil Rights organizer and activist, Bayard Rustin.
1998	I Thought My Soul Would Rise and Fly: The Diary of Patsy, a Freed Girl	Joyce Hansen	Ages 10 and up	Scholastic	The life story of a freed slave.

YEAR	TITLE	AUTHOR	RECOMMENDED READING LEVEL	PUBLISHER/ ISBN	ANNOTATION
1997	Rebels Against Slavery: American Slave Revolts	Patricia C. & Frederick L. McKissack	Ages 12 and up	Scholastic	A tribute to heroes who rebelled against slavery.
1996	The Watsons Go to Birmingham—1963	Christopher Paul Curtis	Ages 9-12	Delacorte	Nine-year-old Kenny tells the story of his African-American middle class family and their trip from Michigan to Alabama.
1996	Like Sisters on the Homefront	Rita Williams-Garcia	Young Adult	Delacorte	The main character is a troubled 14-year-old girl who is sent to live down south with her extended family.
1996	From the Notebooks of Melanin Sun	Jacqueline Woodson	Young Adult	Scholastic/ Blue Sky Press	A story of same sex love and the support of a teenage daughter. Told from a teenager's point of view.
1995	The Captive	Joyce Hansen	Young Adult	Scholastic	When Kofi's father, is killed, Kofi is sold as a slave and ends up in Massachusetts.
1995	I Hadn't Meant to Tell You This	Jacqueline Woodson	Young Adult	Delacorte	A biracial friendship reveals that one of the girls is being treated horribly at home.
1995	Black Diamond: Story of the Negro Baseball League	Patricia C. & Frederick L. McKissack	Ages 12 and up	Scholastic	A historical portrayal of the Negro Baseball League from the beginning to end.
1994	Brown Honey in Broom Wheat Tea	Joyce Carol Thomas, Floyd Cooper (Illustrator)	Ages 4-8	HarperCollins	Poems that speak to African-American children who are trying to find their own identity.
1994	Malcolm X: By Any Means Necessary	Walter Dean Myers	Ages 12 and up	Scholastic	A historical journey of Malcolm X.
1993	Mississippi Challenge	Mildred Pitts	Young Adult	Simon & Schuster Children's Publishing	Nonfiction texts about the history of African Americans.
1993	Sojourner Truth: Ain't I a Woman?	Patricia C. & Frederick L. McKissack	Ages 9-12	Scholastic	Written in 1850, The Narrative of Sojourner Truth is the autobiography of American abolitionist and women's rights activist Sojourner Truth (1797-1883).
1993	Somewhere in the Darkness	Walter Dean Myers	Young Adult	Scholastic	Jimmy and his father, travel the country as Jimmy's father runs from the law.
1992	Night on Neighborhood	Eloise Greenfield, Jan Spivey (Illustrator)	Ages 4-8	Dial	This children's book describes the sights and sounds of one African- American neighborhood at night.
1991	Black Dance in America	James Haskins	Young Adult	Crowell	Presents the history of black dance in America, from its beginnings to modern day.

YEAR	TITLE	AUTHOR	RECOMMENDED READING LEVEL	PUBLISHER/ ISBN	ANNOTATION
1991	*When I Am Old with You*	Angela Johnson	Ages 4-8	Orchard	Told from a child's point of view as she imagines life with Grandpa if she were his age.
1990	*Nathaniel Talking*	Eloise Greenfield, Jan Spivey Gilchrist (Illustrator)	Ages 5-10	Black Butterfly	A collection of poetry in many forms from 9-year-old Nathaniel's point of view.
1990	*The Bells of Christmas*	Virginia Hamilton	Ages 9-12	Harcourt	Twelve-year-old Jason Bell waits impatiently for Christmas 1890. The story describes a middle-class black family during that time in history.
1990	*Martin Luther King, Jr., and the Freedom Movement*	Lillie Patterson	Young Adult	Facts on File	A biography of Martin Luther King, Jr. and his life as a leader.
1989	*A Thief in the Village and Other Stories*	James Berry	Ages 9-12	Orchard	The story of a Jamaican family and their trials and tribulations.
1989	*Anthony Burns: The Defeat and Triumph of a Fugitive Slave*	Virginia Hamilton	Young Adult	Knopf	Biography of Anthony Burns, a 20-year-old black man, was put on trial in Boston under the Fugitive Slave Act of 1850.
1988	*An Enchanted Hair Tale*	Alexis De Veaux	Ages 5-9	HarperCollins	Sudan suffers from the general ridicule of his strange-looking hair, until he comes to accept and enjoy its enchantment.
1988	*The Tales of Uncle Remus: The Adventures of Brer Rabbit*	Julius Lester	Ages 8-12	Penguin Group	These animal tales were collected by Joel Chandler Harris and published between 1896 and 1918.
1987	*Lion and the Ostrich Chicks and Other African Folk Tales*	Ashley Bryan	Ages 7-11	Simon & Schuster Children's Publishing	Includes four traditional tales told by the Hausa, Angolan, Masai, and Bushmen people of Africa.
1987	*Which Way Freedom*	Joyce Hansen	Ages 12 and up	HarperCollins Publishers	Obi escapes from slavery during the Civil War, joins a black Union regiment.
1986	*Junius Over Far*	Virginia Hamilton	Young Adult	HarperCollins Publishers	Junius, a 14-year-old boy follows in his Caribbean grandfather's footsteps.
1986	*Trouble's Child*	Mildred Pitts	Ages 9-12	William Morrow & Co.	Martha dreams of attending high school and becoming something.
1985	*Circle of Gold*	Candy Dawson Boyd	Ages 9-12	Scholastic	Mattie's world changes when her father dies and her mother becomes someone she doesn't recognize.

YEAR	TITLE	AUTHOR	RECOMMENDED READING LEVEL	PUBLISHER	ANNOTATION
1985	*A Little Love*	Virginia Hamilton	Young Adult	Penguin Group	Raised by her devoted grand-parents, a teen searches for her father.
1984	*The Magical Adventures of Pretty Pearl*	Virginia Hamilton	Ages 9-12	HarperCollins	Pretty Pearl is a god among mortals.
1984	*Lena Horne*	James Haskins	Ages 12 and up	Penguin Group	A biography of Lean Horne.
1984	*Bright Shadow*	Joyce Carol Thomas		HarperCollins	A town must learn to cope when a young man goes missing.
1984	*Because We Are*	Mildred Pitts Walter	Ages 11 and up	HarperCollins	Emma is transferred from an integrated school to a segregated school after a misunderstanding with a teacher.
1983	*This Strange New Feeling*	Julius Lester	Young Adult	Dial	Slave histories that are insightful and poignant.
1982	*Rainbow Jordan*	Alice Childress	Young Adult	HarperCollins	Rainbow Jordan prepares to go to yet another foster home.
1982	*Lou in the Limelight*	Kristine Hunter	Ages 12 and up	Macmillan Publishing Company	A cautionary tale of young men trying to make it in the music business.
1982	*Mary: An Autobiography*	Mary E. Mebane	Ages 12 and up	Viking	The autobiography of Mary Mebane and her life in rural black America.
1981	*Don't Explain: A Song of Billie Holiday*	Alexis De Veaux	Young Adult	HarperCollins Children's Books	A prose poem about legendary Billie Holiday.
1980	*Movin' Up*	Berry Gordy	Ages 10 and up	HarperCollins	The autobiography of Berry Gordy, Sr., son of a slave and father of the founder of Motown Records.
1980	*Childtimes: A Three-Generation Memoir*	Eloise Greenfield and Lessie Jones Little	Ages 12 and up	HarperCollins	A collection of stories from three black women's perspectives.
1980	*Andrew Young: Young Man with a Mission*	James Haskins	Ages 12 and up	Lothrop	The life story of Andrew Young, U.S. Ambassador to the United Nations.
1980	*James Van Der Zee: The Picture Takin' Man*	James Haskins	Young Adult	Africa World Press	Biography of James Van Der Zee.
1980	*Let the Lion Eat Straw*	Ellease Southerland	Young Adult	HarperCollins	Story of a young lady who flees poverty in the South for opportunities in the North.
1979	*Benjamin Banneker*	Lillie Patterson	Ages 8-12	Abingdon Press	The history of the scientist Benjamin Banneker.
1979	*I Have a Sister, My Sister is Deaf*	Jeanne W. Peterson	Ages 4-8	HarperTrophy	The story of a sister of a deaf girl.

YEAR	TITLE	AUTHOR	RECOMMENDED READING LEVEL	PUBLISHER/ ISBN	ANNOTATION
1979	*Justice and Her Brothers*	Virginia Hamilton	Young Adult	HarperCollins Publishers	A story of twins and their sensory perceptions.
1979	*Skates of Uncle Richard*	Carol Fenner	Ages 7-10	Random House Books for Young Readers	With the love and encouragement of her uncle, a young girl dares to follow her dream to become a figure skater.
1978	*The Days When the Animals Talked: Black Folk Tales and How They Came to Be*	William J. Faulkner	Ages 9-12	Follett	Features more than 20 African-American folktales.
1978	*Marvin and Tige*	Frankcina Glass	Young Adult	Random House Publishing Group	Two unlikely friends who differ in race and age become allies in life.
1978	*Mary McCleod Bethune*	Eloise Greenfield	Ages 5-9	HarperCollins Children's Books	The biography of Mary McCleod Bethune.
1978	*Barbara Jordan*	James Haskins	Ages 12 and up	Dial	The story of Texas's first black senator in Congress serving two terms.
1978	*Coretta Scott King*	Lillie Patterson	Ages 9 and up	Garrard	The life story of the widow of Martin Luther King, Jr.
1978	*Portia: The Life of Portia Washington Pittman, the Daughter of Booker T. Washington*	Ruth Ann Stewart	Ages 9 and up	Doubleday	A biography about the daughter of Booker T. Washington.

Bibliography

American Library Association. (2008). *Award Winners and Honors*. Retrieved September 9, 2008 from <http://www.ala.org/ala/mgrps/rts/emiert/corettascottkingbookaward/cskwinners/cskpastwinners/cskpastwinners.cfm>.

American Red Cross (2008). *Facing Personal Feelings*. Retrieved September 1, 2008 from <http://www.neahin.org/programs/schoolsafety/resources/materials/rl01.htm>.

Anderson, R., Wilson, P., & Fielding, L. (1988). Growth in reading and how children spend their time outside of school. *Reading Research Quarterly*, Summer, 65-78.

Baer, F. C. (2001). *Creative Proverbs from African-American Culture*. Retrieved September 4, 2008 from <http://creativeproverbs.com/az01.htm>.

Bernadowski, C. (October 2008). Aren't we all teachers of literacy? *Library Media Connection*, 28-29.

Corporation for Public Broadcasting. (2005). *African-American World*. Retrieved October 10, 2008 from <http://www.pbs.org/wnet/aaworld/credits.html>.

Draper, Sharon. (2008). *Welcome to Sharon Draper.com*. Retrieved July 20, 2008 from <http://sharondraper.com>.

Elfner, L. E. (2002). *Adventures of Cyberbee*. How to Write a Business Letter. Retrieved on August 21, 2008 from <http://www.cyberbee.com/science/letpart.html>.

Gambrell, L. B., & Almasi, J. F. (1996). *Lively discussions: Fostering engaged reading*. Newark, DE: International Reading Association.

Hamilton Arts Inc. (2001). *Virginia Hamilton: Welcome to My World*. Retrieved July 4, 2008 from <http://www.virginiahamilton.com/home.htm>.

Harris Middle School Teachers. (2004). Evaluation Plan for Letters. Retrieved July 6, 2008 from <http://canadaonline.about.com/gi/dynamic/offsite.htm?site=http%3A%2F%2Fvolweb.ut k.edu%2FSchools%2Fbedford%2Fharrisms%2Fletterrubric.htm>.

Mildred Pitts Walter. (2008). Colorado Women Hall of Fame. Retrieved June 30, 2008 from <http://www.cogreatwomen.org/walter.htm>.

Mildred Teacher Resource File. (2000). *Index to Internet Sites: Children's and Young Adults' Authors & Illustrators*. Retrieved on October 31, 2008 from <http://falcon.jmu.edu/~ramseyil/taylor.htm>.

Raphael, T., & Au, K. (2005). QAR: Enhancing comprehension and test taking across grade and content areas. *The Reading Teacher, 59*, 206-221.

Raphael, T., Highfield, K., & Au, K. (2006). *QAR now: a powerful and practical framework that develops comprehension and higher-level thinking in all students*. New York: Scholastic.

Raphael, T. E. (1982). Teaching children question-answering strategies. *The Reading Teacher, 36,* 186-191.

Raphael, T. E. (1986). Teaching children question-answering relationships, revisited. *The Reading Teacher, 39,* 516-522.

Raphael, T. E. (1984). Teaching learners about sources of information for answering questions. *Journal of Reading, 27,* 303-311.

Taylor, Mildred D. (2007). *The Mississippi Writers Page.* The University of Mississippi English Department. Retrieved October 1, 2008 from <http://www.olemiss.edu/mwp/dir/taylor_mildred>.

The University of Wisconsin, Madison. (2007). Cooperative Children's Book Center. Retrieved September 3, 2008 from <http://www.education.wisc.edu/ccbc/>.

Zemelman, S., Daniels, H., & Hyde, A. (1993). *Best practice: New standards for teaching and learning in America's schools.* Portsmouth, NH: Heinemann.

Author Index

C

Clifton, Lucille, 25-31

D

Draper, Sharon, 119-24

Duckett, Alfred, 3-14

H

Hamilton, Virginia, 33-44

J

Johnson, Angela, 85-93, 103-7, 109-18

M

Myers, Walter Dean, 17-24, 57-69, 95-100

R

Robinson, Jackie, 3-16

T

Taylor, Mildred D., 71-83

W

Walter, Mildred Pitts, 45-57

Title Index

C

Copper Sun, xix, 21-26

E

Everett Anderson's Goodbye, xvii, 25-31

F

Fallen Angels, xviii, 59-70

H

Heaven, viii, xviii, 103-108

I

I Never Had It Made: The Autobiography of Jackie Robinson, xvii, 3-16

J

Justin and the Best Biscuits in the World, xvii, 45-57

S

Slam!, xviii, 95-100

T

The First Part Last, xix, 21-20

The People Could Fly: American Black Folktales, xvii, 33-44

The Road to Memphis, xviii, 71-83

The Young Landlords, xvii, 17-24

Toning the Sweep, xviii, 85-93, 118

Subject Index

A

Anticipation guide, 88, 89

B

Black cowboys, 55
Booktalk, 80, 82
Business letter, 17, 18

C

Cooperative Children's Book Center,
 x, xi, xii, xvii-xix
Coretta Scott King Award, x-xi, xiii

E

Emancipation Proclamation, 120

F

Family tree, 47, 48
Folktales, 31-32, 34, 38

H

Haiku, 25-26, 27
Harlem, 15, 20, 22, 96, 102

I

Information Literacy Standards for
 Student Learning, x, xv, xvi, xvii-xix

J

Journal writing, 34, 86, 123

K

KWL, 58, 59, 67
KWLQ, 4, 5

L

Literature circles, xviii, 96-97

N

NCTE/IRA Standards for the English
 Language Arts, x, xii, xv-xvi,
 xvii-xix

Q

Question-Answer relationship, 75

R

Readers Theatre, 22, 41
Research
 dream job, 96
 names, 106
 slavery, 32, 120, 124

S

Similes, 49
Slave narratives, 39, 42
Slavery, 32, 120, 124

V

Venn diagram, 51, 52
Vietnam War, 57-58, 59, 65, 67, 68
Vocabulary, xv, 60, 72, 91, 113

W

Word webs, 16